The **Covenants,**
Christ, and
You

Ryan Churchill

Andrew Kirschner, Editor

The Covenants, Christ, and You
Copyright © 2015 Ryan Churchill
www.thecovenantschristandyou.com

Published by Vassal Press
Carl Junction, MO

Vassal Press was created for the sole purpose of publishing
The Covenants, Christ, and You and any future books by Ryan Churchill.
Please contact Vassal Press at www.thecovenantschristandyou.com with any questions.

First edition: July, 2015

BISAC: REL006000

ISBN: 978-0-9964876-0-3 (sc)

Also available in various eBook formats

Printed in the United States of America

Readers should be aware that Internet Web sites offered as citations and/or sources for further information may have changed or disappeared between the time this was written and when it is read.

Cover design by Ryan Churchill

Modified istockphoto.com #000013963675 using picmonkey.com software

Interior Illustrations by Naomi Miller, Copyright © 2015 Used by Permission

Proofreading, page design and typesetting by D&S Pre-Press Services
dands.pp.serv@gmail.com

Soli Deo Gloria

. . . for I will forgive their iniquity,
and their sins I will remember no more.
—Jeremiah 31:34

Table of Contents

Preface
How to use this book

The Covenants, Christ, and You is a Bible study in the form of a workbook. As I was writing this study, I had four situations I was targeting for practical application. It is not limited to these four situations, but these are the targets at which I was aiming:

- Small Group Bible Study or Classroom Setting (i.e., Sunday School)
- Personal Bible Study
- Transformation Group, a group of three to four people who get together and discuss the Word of God on a weekly or bi-weekly basis.
- Discipleship training or Home School (grades 8-12)

A note to group and class leaders

In terms of a group being led by a leader, I would respectfully ask that leaders complete *The Covenants, Christ, and You* as a personal study prior to implementing it in the larger group. At the very least, you should be one or two chapters ahead of your group. The book is broken down into topics but not lessons. Whereas it may be feasible to complete the first chapter in one regular meeting, it won't necessarily be a possibility for the fourth chapter. Group leaders should teach at their own pace and at a pace appropriate to the class. I highly recommend asking participants in the class to complete a whole chapter as personal study throughout the week, and then as a group, discuss questions and reflect on the study. Group leaders should set goals for the weekly discussions, but keep in mind that preparation allows for you to be flexible.

Preface

This said, you know your participants better than I. If you would rather read through it as a group and discuss and write as you go, this will work for that purpose as well. Regardless of your approach, make sure that as you set goals you are willing to yield to the spiritual needs of the moment.

Personal Bible Study

I really love *The Covenants, Christ, and You* as a personal Bible study—ultimately, while I was writing, that is what it was for me. This book isn't about your knowing the right answers. There is no answer key. It is intended for the purpose of guiding you through God's Word as He revealed Himself through the covenants. Please proceed prayerfully.

If you are not a believer and you are picking this book up out of curiosity, I'm glad! I hope *The Covenants, Christ, and You* leads you into greater understanding of who God reveals Himself to be and that He intends to have a relationship with you. I pray that you find what you need in God's Word. You will need a Bible, and if you don't have one, I used the following link to get to every Scripture for this study: http://biblehub.com/nasb/ (February 2015). There are plenty of free Bible resources to make this possible for you.

If this book blesses you, I would very much appreciate your spreading the word about it. I believe *The Covenants, Christ, and You* is intended for a vast audience, and there are seekers in this world waiting for you to share. I encourage you to find someone, get them a copy, and enthusiastically offer to go through the book with them. So often, we look to do big things for God. Often, it is the smallest gesture that makes the greatest impact. While I'm all for doing things to honor God in my life, I find that the greatest moments occur not when I'm doing something FOR Him but instead when I am WITH Him. I hope *The Covenants, Christ, and You* will be a "with Him" experience.

Transformation Group and Discipleship Training

Ultimately, by taking your personal study time and sitting down with someone else to engage in the Word of God, you're doing discipleship and you're participating in transformation. It is God's Word that transforms us. *The Covenants, Christ, and You* is designed to invest you in, direct you to, and guide you through God's Word. You will find many Scriptures that you need to look up, think about, pray about, and respond to before you move on. If you are participating in a transformation group or discipleship training, you must put in the time outside of group time. Enter group time prepared to share.

Final thoughts before we begin

I am hesitant to use this word, as you may see it and close the book. Before you close the book, hear me out. What you're about to encounter is theology. BUT, it is practical theology. The contents of this book will be nothing new to a person who has completed seminary. *The Covenants, Christ, and You* is a practical look at the covenants that can be applied to our every-day lives. "Theology" is a word that is often feared, but it doesn't need to be. You'll hardly even notice that you're learning theology. Instead, I hope you will notice that you're learning God the Father, God the Son, and God the Holy Spirit. Understanding covenant will provide a new and powerful lens through which you can view Scripture. It can prove helpful in understanding some of the really tough questions you have when looking at Scripture. Though it won't necessarily illuminate everything, covenant understanding can shine a light on numerous difficult passages.

If you are fairly familiar with the Bible, I would like to present a challenge for you. I would like you to choose two passages (in their larger context) out of the Bible that really challenge your understanding (if this is all new to you, don't worry about this challenge). Choose one from the Old Testament and choose one of Jesus' actions or teachings, for instance, a difficult parable. Write them down on the two lines below. At the end of your study, come back and revisit these two passages. My hope is that you will have a different lens through which you can explore these passages, and perhaps, you can increase in your understanding or find peace that surpasses understanding, trusting that one day all will be illuminated.

_____

_____

Intro Chapter

Covenant Introduction

This cup is the new covenant in My blood;
do this, as often as you drink it, in remembrance of Me.

—1 Corinthians 11:25

"Do This In Remembrance of Me." These words are inscribed on almost every communion table I have ever seen. And so, that's what I learned to do at communion. I remembered Jesus. It actually seems odd to think of it that way now. Despite all the artistic renderings, I don't have a clue what He looks like. I've never heard Him audibly speak. I wasn't actually at the Last Supper. How can it be that I should remember Him? These words plagued my communion time for years. I knew Jesus died to forgive my sin. I appreciated that, and when I had been especially awful, communion had more meaning as I could let go of the sins, remembering what Jesus accomplished at the cross. If it had been a good week, though, there just didn't seem to be much point in communion, other than being a real downer after a couple of up-tempo praise tunes.

I must admit there were a couple of words that always stuck out during communion for some reason. I never had much depth of understanding for two words in particular that Jesus said while instituting the Lord's Supper, but what little understanding I did have made them seem important. The two words? New Covenant. It wasn't so much the word "new" as much as the word "covenant" that grabbed me. Somehow though, I realized that the word "new" was pretty important, too.

"Covenant" is a word we throw around a lot in Christianity, and we pretend everyone understands it. It sort of gets covered during the time when we prepare kids for baptism or maybe dur-

Covenant Introduction

ing confirmation classes. It is rightfully a part of our marriage vocabulary as well. For some reason though, we treat these occurrences of "covenant" in the same regard as "contract." As I was only a few weeks into my study of the covenants, God placed me in a situation where covenant and contract were contrasted. Here is the illustration my friend, Adam, presented:

Contract: Imagine you are going to purchase a cup of coffee at AllYerBucks. If you hand four dollars to the guy behind the counter, he hands you a large mocha. If you don't have four dollars, he doesn't give you a large mocha. Likewise, if he doesn't have a large mocha, you don't hand him your four dollars.

Covenant: Imagine you're going to AllYerBucks coffee again. The coffee still costs four dollars. It is still understood that the guy at the counter will hand you a large mocha when you hand him four dollars. Here's where things are different from contract. If you don't have four dollars, the guy at the counter still hands you a large mocha. Also, you may have your four dollars, but he doesn't have a large mocha for you. Yet you still give him your four dollars.[1]

With contract, you have an impersonal exchange of goods and services. On the other hand with covenants, you establish relationship. In covenant, the two participants tell one another, "Everything I have, and everything that I am is yours."

It isn't very likely that you're going to be entering into a covenant relationship with your local barista, so let's look at a different rendering of covenant based on two people with goods, rather than one with money and the other possessing goods, to see how this actually works. I'm going to use livestock as the commodity at the center of this covenant, as that would have been a very typical purpose behind a covenant between two parties in the Old Testament times. Contracts are secured on signed pieces of paper or with a firm handshake whereas Old Testament covenants were secured in blood.

If you are studying this in a small group, you may want to have two people from the small group act this out, and you may substitute their first names.

Imagine Joe Goatherd (The Goat Herder) and Steven Cowherd (The Cattle Man) wanted to enter covenant. The two would take a few animals, likely a cow and a goat, and they would cut the animals in half. This is not a cut in the torso, but instead, this is bisection, meaning they cut the animals in half from tip of the nose to tail. Then the two (or more) animals would be laid out on the ground with their left and right halves separated from one another by a space that the two participants could walk through.

As you can imagine, the act of cutting the animals releases a great deal of blood, which falls to the ground between the bisected halves. So, you have a corridor of blood separating the halves. Each man stands at opposite ends of the corridor. Joe Goatherd at one end and Steven Cowherd at the other end. Then, the two men walk through the corridor of blood and end up on opposite ends. The understanding at this point is that they are now joined together in covenant.

By passing through the blood, they have told one another, "Everything I have, and everything that I am, is yours." Additionally, they are telling each other, "If I break this covenant, the fate these animals have experienced will also happen to me." (Yikes!) The result of this agreement means Steven is not only going to watch over his herd of cattle, he will also protect Joe's goats. Likewise, Joe will watch over Steven's cattle in addition to his goat herding duties. Furthermore, if Steven needs a goat, he has many to choose from at this point. Likewise, Joe has many cattle to choose from.

So far, this just looks like a very grotesque way to establish a contract, but covenant extends beyond the point of contract. Not only did they join their commodities, they joined their identities. Joe is no longer, Joe Goatherd. He is now Joe Goatherd-Cowherd. Likewise, Steven is no longer Steven Cowherd. He is now Steven Cowherd-Goatherd. Remember, the statement they made by passing through the halves went beyond "everything I have." It extended to "everything that I am." This is an adoption of identity. Everyone in the land would know about this covenant. Everyone would know that stealing from Joe meant that not only Joe's family would be coming after them, Steven's family would be coming too, because the two families are now one.

When two people, or two families, enter covenant, they establish relationship. In relationship, we have responsibilities. Conversely, in contract, we have contingencies. Regardless of what the other person is bringing to the relationship, we still act out of responsibility. In contract, we act only if the other person is prepared to act.

As mentioned above, I never fully understood covenant. It seemed important, but I didn't fully grasp it. Covenant is a word that makes a lot of sense in some cultures, but has a vague meaning in other cultures. Let's simplify this word. Covenant is relationship. I'm going to toss in one other word at this point because we've talked about responsibility. In Christian vernacular, there is a word we use that means responsibility, but we don't really notice it. In fact, the use of this word in two similar, but different, phrases has created a lot of complicated theories. The word: kingdom. Let's simplify this word. As a believer in Christ, and one who is submitted to His will, you have kingdom responsibilities. You see this word used by Jesus and John the Baptist. When they say, "the kingdom of Heaven" or "the kingdom of God" is at hand, they are admonishing people to start acting on their responsibilities.

Thus far, we've been dealing with covenants as they relate to two equal parties. For example, if I had a dispute with my mortgage lender, I could take my lender to court. Standing before the

Covenant Introduction

judge, we would have our arguments equally heard and equally considered. This is because we both bring the same sort of value to the relationship. They supplied money to purchase my house, and I am using money to pay them back.

Biblical covenants, those between God and humans, are not between two equal parties. Biblical covenants are known as "suzerain-vassal" covenants. The suzerain is the stronger party and the vassal is the weaker party. (I promise, I won't keep using million dollar words throughout the study, but it matters here.) The vassal enters into covenant with the suzerain by offering devotion and loyalty to the suzerain, while the suzerain offers protection and privilege to the vassal. Oversimplifying this and going back to the Large Mocha illustration, the suzerain says to the vassal, "There is nothing you can pay that is worthy of this Large Mocha, but I give it to you anyway because you asked and have committed to becoming devoted and loyal to me. I'm glad you now realize I always love you and I want to be a blessing to you."[2]

The identity part of the suzerain-vassal covenant is not the same as a covenant between two equal parties. The exchange occurs, but it occurs differently. Let's look at the identity exchange in the New Covenant. Jesus (the suzerain) enters the covenant as Jesus Holy. We (the vassal) enter the covenant as _____{Insert your name}_____ Sinner. Having entered covenant, we give up the last name, Sinner. We become _____{Insert your name}_____ Holy. Jesus, however, remains Jesus Holy. That isn't to say He didn't receive our name, Sinner. He took our identity, sinner, and our sins were upon Him as He hung on the cross. He took all our sins as He passed through death; and when He conquered the grave, He abolished the penalty we owe for our sins. Now, He is Jesus, Lord of _____{Insert your name}_____. This is much like Abraham belonging to God and God identifying Himself as The God of Abraham.

There are seven Biblical instances where God established covenant with mankind. Admittedly, in the first two instances, God does not use the term covenant. He does, however, use covenant language in these two instances, and He establishes relationship. The first six covenants were established in the Old Testament and the final covenant, the New Covenant, was established in the New Testament. Now that we have an introduction into covenant, you may be saying, "Now that I get this, there doesn't seem to be much else that matters." You may be questioning, "What is the point of going through all these covenants?" "Is this just going to be about gathering information so I can sound smart?" "What relevance can some Old Testament covenants have for me?"

I promise you, this isn't about information gathering. You will get a lot of information, but that won't be the point. On the road to Emmaus, Jesus, the resurrected Christ, appeared to two mournful disciples. Luke tells us, ". . . beginning with Moses and with all the prophets, He explained to them the things concerning Himself in all the Scriptures." (Luke 24:27) If Jesus is in all the

Scriptures, He must be present in all the covenants. In *The Covenants, Christ, and You*, we're going to go on a journey to discover the presence of Jesus in God's establishment of covenant. We're going to discover how God revealed Himself to humanity and who He revealed humanity to be. Finally, we're going to discover how these covenants are still relevant in, and pertinent to, our twenty-first century lives. In the words of Jesus. Follow me.

Chapter 1

The Edenic Covenant

*From any tree of the garden you may eat freely; but from the tree of the
knowledge of good and evil you shall not eat, for in the day
that you eat from it you will surely die.*

—Genesis 2:16-17

How difficult could it have been? Don't you wish you could ask Adam and Eve that one simple question? When compared to the temptations of today, avoiding one little fruit doesn't sound like too difficult a task. The story of Adam and Eve is a story with which almost any Christian will be familiar. Even non-Christians are fairly well versed in the story about the fall of mankind. In our society, it is used as a way to teach everyone that we're imperfect. On the flip side: It is used by some as an example of an allegorical story written by some man who just wanted to oppress women. For some, it has inspired great works of art.

I personally have a difficult time believing God would have this story line written into His holy Scripture if there wasn't a greater lesson to be learned. You see, the Old Testament is a love letter from a Creator addressed to His fallen creation. He yearns greatly for His creation to turn back to Him. In the story of Eden, God provides three very important revelations: 1. He reveals Himself to humanity, 2. He reveals His intentions for humanity and, 3. He reveals His intention for relationship with His creation. God never refers to a covenant in Eden, but He does give a command, which, if broken, would lead to a deadly consequence. This command is known as the Edenic Covenant.

The Edenic Covenant

Genesis 2:4-9,15-22

[1]*Thus the heavens and the earth were completed, and all their hosts.* [2]*By the seventh day God completed His work which He had done, and He rested on the seventh day from all His work which He had done.* [3]*Then God blessed the seventh day and sanctified it, because in it He rested from all His work which God had created and made.* [4]*This is the account of the heavens and the earth when they were created, in the day that the LORD God made earth and heaven.* [5]*Now no shrub of the field was yet in the earth, and no plant of the field had yet sprouted, for the LORD God had not sent rain upon the earth, and there was no man to cultivate the ground.* [6]*But a mist used to rise from the earth and water the whole surface of the ground.* [7]*Then the LORD God formed man of dust from the ground, and breathed into his nostrils the breath of life; and man became a living being.* [8]*The LORD God planted a garden toward the east, in Eden; and there He placed the man whom He had formed.* [9]*Out of the ground the LORD God caused to grow every tree that is pleasing to the sight and good for food; the tree of life also in the midst of the garden, and the tree of the knowledge of good and evil. . . .* [15]*Then the LORD God took the man and put him into the garden of Eden to cultivate it and keep it.* [16]*The LORD God commanded the man, saying, "From any tree of the garden you may eat freely;* [17]*but from the tree of the knowledge of good and evil you shall not eat, for in the day that you eat from it you will surely die."* [18]*Then the LORD God said, "It is not good for the man to be alone; I will make him a helper suitable for him."* [19]*Out of the ground the LORD God formed every beast of the field and every bird of the sky, and brought them to the man to see what he would call them; and whatever the man called a living creature, that was its name.* [20]*The man gave names to all the cattle, and to the birds of the sky, and to every beast of the field, but for Adam there was not found a helper suitable for him.* [21]*So the LORD God caused a deep sleep to fall upon the man, and he slept; then He took one of his ribs and closed up the flesh at that place.* [22]*The LORD God fashioned into a woman the rib which He had taken from the man, and brought her to the man.*

Write out the command God gave Adam in the Edenic covenant? (v. 16)

_____

_____

What consequence does God tell Adam he will experience if the covenant is broken?

_____

_____

Most people are quick to recognize that God essentially said, "Don't eat from the tree of knowledge of good and evil." What we often fail to realize is that God commanded Adam to "eat freely" from all the other trees. Of particular interest to me is the fact that God first commanded

Adam to eat freely, thus revealing to Adam that He (God) is, first and foremost, the great provider . . . not the great withholder.

Read carefully the final part of the command that God gave Adam. What does this tell you about God's intention for Adam's lifespan? (v. 17)

_____

_____

As a human being, Adam was created to be an eternal being. Read Genesis 1:27. If God created man in His own image, and Adam was created to be an eternal being, what does that tell you about the nature of God?

_____

_____

Read verses 19 and 20. List the responsibilities God gave Adam.

_____

_____

How did Adam encounter the animals?

_____

Would you describe Adam as working *for* God or working *with* God? What is the difference between working for God and working with God?

_____

_____

God noted that something was not good, what was it?

_____

Read Genesis 1:26. God said, "Let <u>US</u> make man in <u>Our</u> image." In this statement, we can see why it was not good that man was alone if he was created in the image of God. In Genesis 1:26, we can see that God is not a lonely singular being. In the Trinity— Father, Son, and Holy Spirit— God is a self-contained community.

The Edenic Covenant

Summarize the following verses:

John 14:31

_____

John 14:23-24

_____

For what purpose do you believe God placed the tree of knowledge of good and evil in the garden?

_____

_____

So much attention is placed on the term "free will" when talking about the tree of knowledge of good and evil. It should be noted that while "free will" is an observable conclusion, much like the "Trinity," neither "free will" nor "Trinity" can be found as terminology in the Bible. What is noted in the Bible is the term "obedience." Saying "yes" to God is the ultimate way of loving and honoring Him. We cannot be in His presence, without showing Him honor. Obedience is the act of freely choosing God's will above our own will.

The Fall   As we all know, Adam and Eve did not remain in the paradise called Eden. They were cast out of the garden as a consequence for falling into sin. I think few people can read this story without trying, to some degree, to imagine what life must have been like in the garden prior to the fall. It is difficult to come up with a clear image. A life without worry? A life without anxiety? A life without death? A life without shame? A life fully dependent on God? A life where the only thing you need is God? When we superimpose our current reality, the human mind will find this life lived in the garden to be unimaginable and unattainable. For Adam and Eve, however, this life was all they knew before the fall. Their lives were unclouded by sin, and being in God's presence was common, natural, and simple. Sadly, eating from the tree of knowledge turned humanity's clear view of their Creator into a dim reflection, as in a mirror (1 Cor. 13:12).

Because of the failure of Adam and Eve, we are born into a life where our reality is a world saturated in sin and separate from God. We are born into a world of shame, instinctually hiding aspects of our lives, leading to deception so as not to be judged too harshly by our critics. When we look at Adam and Eve, it is frustrating to see how perfect their lives were and wonder how it was that they fell into the trap of crossing the one boundary set before them. It seemed like such a simple instruction: you can eat anything you want from all the fruits in the garden, except, don't eat from this tree. How could they possibly mess up one simple rule? In order to understand the answer to this question, you have to have an understanding of how Satan operates.

Take a look at the following verses regarding Adam and Eve's command and temptation, followed by verses regarding Jesus' baptism and temptation in the wilderness. Write down the contradiction you see between the two excerpts from Genesis. Likewise, write down the contradiction you see between the two chapters from Luke.

Genesis 2:17 and Genesis 3:4-5

_____

_____

Luke 3:22, Luke 4:3, and Luke 4:9.

_____

_____

Read John 8:44. What do all these verses reveal about the nature of Satan?

_____

The first thing Satan did was challenge God's spoken Word. He told Adam and Eve, "You surely won't die." He said to Jesus, "*IF* You are the Son of God. . . ." Satan's most common weapon is the seed of doubt. He will inherently contradict the Word of God. When Satan speaks, he speaks lies.

There is a deeper dimension in Satan's tactics. The tactic is rooted in his use of the word "If." Notice that Satan immediately attacked God's proclamation of Jesus as The Son of God. Satan attacked Jesus' God-given identity. Likewise, he told Eve, "For God knows that in the day you eat from it your eyes will be opened, and *you will be like God*, knowing good and evil." (Gen. 3:5) In this statement, Satan refuted God's proclamation that He created mankind in His own image. Satan doesn't put sin at the heart of temptation, he places your identity at the heart of temptation. He wants you to believe his lies about who you are, instead of accepting the truth of who God reveals you to be.

Read Genesis 3:1-3; and then re-read God's covenant command (Gen. 2:16-17). What did Eve reveal to the serpent about her knowledge of God's Word, which gave him the opportunity to plant the seed of doubt?

_____

_____

The Edenic Covenant

When we fail to know God's Word, we leave the door open for doubt to enter our minds and hearts. The serpent merely had to touch the fruit to disprove Eve's understanding of God's Word.

Satan may have won the battle in the garden with Adam and Eve, but he took a loss when the playing field was moved to the desert and his opponent was Jesus. In 1 Corinthians 15:45, Paul refers to Jesus as "the last Adam." Did Jesus have an advantage over Adam? Jesus was in close relationship with the Father, true, but one could easily say the same of Adam.

Christ in the Covenant

In just a few words, write down what the following verses reveal about Jesus:

Isaiah 53:1-3

_____

_____

Mathew 4:2

_____

_____

Luke 2:52

_____

_____

John 4:4-7

_____

_____

John 11:35

_____

_____

Hebrews 2:17

_____

_____

Matthew 13:53-58

_____

_____

Luke 22:41-44

_____

_____

Based on what you know about Jesus, how does the life of Jesus, and how He lived it, compare with the life of Adam before the fall?

_____

_____

_____

I believe there is a tendency to superimpose the picture of the garden onto Jesus' perfectly sinless life and assume He had a perfect life. In terms of sin, He was perfect in that He was sinless. However, Jesus' life was far from perfect. His friend Lazarus passed away and He wept. He was mocked. He lived His ministerial life fleeing from religious authorities who wanted to capture Him. When He returned to His hometown, He was without honor. Jesus was greatly stressed at the thought of His pending death. In the garden of Gethsemane, He was sweating blood as He asked that the cup pass from Him. Jesus was fully immersed in life as we know it in a post-Eden world. He did not live an easy life, but He did live a life fully dependent on, and obedient to, His heavenly Father. Regardless of all the realities of humanity, Jesus always chose obedience. Saying "Yes" to the Father was His default response, even becoming obedient to the point of death on the cross (Phil. 2:8).

Read Genesis 3:8-10; Luke 5:16; Mark 1:35; Luke 22:39. What impression do you have of how often Adam communicated with God? How does this compare with how often Jesus communicated with God?

_____

_____

_____

It would seem that Adam and Eve could daily expect to be in contact with God. They knew full well the sound of God walking through the garden. It was a familiar sound to them. Jesus was fully dedicated to His heavenly Father. He regularly communicated with His Father, slipping away to a place of solitude where He could be in prayer, fully experiencing the presence of God.

As you close your lesson today, consider the prayer life of Jesus and then consider Adam and Eve in their fallen state. Do you find yourself actively seeking the presence of God or do you more often find yourself hiding behind the bushes in your shame?

_____

_____

The Edenic Covenant

As we hide in the bushes in our sin and our shame, what does the Lord God call out? See Genesis 3:9.

_____

_____

God Calls   God knew the answer to His question before He called out, "Where are you?" Notice, He doesn't begin with a question of condemnation. Instead, He does here what He has continued to do throughout human history. He actively seeks His people. Once we respond, it won't always be easy. He may follow up with a question leading to confession and repentance. The beauty of confession and repentance is that you'll always find God waiting for you on the other side.

Closing Reflections

What does God reveal about Himself in the Edenic covenant?

What does God reveal about His intentions for humanity?

What does God reveal about His intention for relationship with you?

_____

Join the Conversation on:

Facebook: facebook.com/Thecovenantschristandyou Like and Post your thoughts on God's covenant in Eden

   or

Twitter: @CovChristU Tweet your thoughts on God's covenant in Eden

Engaging Others:

Small Groups or Sunday School Classes: Each member Tweet it, Post it, Pin it, or Instagram a picture of your small group leader leading your discussion of *The Covenants, Christ, and You.* Tweet it to @CovChristU or Tag the Facebook page.

Individuals and Discipleship: Tweet it, Post it, Pin it, or Instagram a picture of an object in your surroundings while you studied *The Covenants, Christ, and You...* (i.e. cup of coffee, Bible, pen, table, chair...) Tweet it to @CovChristU or Tag the Facebook page.

Suggested Hashtags

#Discipleship #ChristFollower #BibleStudy #SmallGroup #Evangelism #Relevant #Jesus

If you're not on social media, with whom can you share this study?

Chapter 2
The Adamic Covenant

He shall bruise you on the head, And you shall bruise him on the heel.

—Genesis 3:15

In the Edenic covenant, God revealed that we were created in His image. He established relationship with Adam and Eve, giving them purpose and responsibility. The three were in perfect relationship. Sadly, at the moment they ate of the fruit, Adam and Eve broke the Edenic Covenant and separated themselves from their Creator. While the imprint of God's image was upon humans and remains thus, in the choice to sin, the clarity of His image in humanity became dull, clouded by sin. The Edenic covenant was broken and a fresh covenant became necessary. In the Adamic covenant, we are going to see God's corrective actions to maintain the relationship He established with His creation. It is a storyline that is familiar to many of us, but to make sure we are all operating from the same storyline, let's read the Biblical account found in the 3rd Chapter of Genesis.

Genesis 3:1-13

¹Now the serpent was more crafty than any beast of the field which the LORD God had made. And he said to the woman, "Indeed, has God said, 'You shall not eat from any tree of the garden'?" ²The woman said to the serpent, "From the fruit of the trees of the garden we may eat; ³but from the fruit of the tree which is in the middle of the garden, God has said, 'You shall not eat from it or touch it, or you will die.'" ⁴The serpent said to the woman, "You surely will not die! ⁵"For God knows that in the day you eat from it your eyes will be opened, and you will be like God, knowing good and evil." ⁶When the woman saw that the tree was good for food, and that it was a delight to the eyes, and that the tree was desirable to make one wise, she took from its fruit and ate; and she gave also to her husband with her, and he ate. [7] Then the eyes of both of them were opened, and they knew that they were naked; and they sewed fig leaves together and made themselves loin coverings.

[8] They heard the sound of the LORD God walking in the garden in the cool of the day, and the man and his wife hid themselves from the presence of the LORD God among the trees of the garden. [9] Then the LORD God called to the man, and said to him, "Where are you?" [10] He said, "I heard the sound of You in the garden, and I was afraid because I was naked; so I hid myself." [11] And He said, "Who told you that you were naked? Have you eaten from the tree of which I commanded you not to eat?" [12] The man said, "The woman whom You gave to be with me, she gave me from the tree, and I ate." [13] Then the LORD God said to the woman, "What is this you have done?" And the woman said, "The serpent deceived me, and I ate."

It is important to note the order of events. Let's condense the order into some short statements:

- The serpent questions the Lord God's command, twisting His words.

- Eve states God's command regarding the fruit of the tree in the middle of the garden.

- The serpent contradicts God and attempts to justify his contradiction.

- Eve eats of the fruit.

- Eve gives the fruit to Adam.

- Adam eats the fruit.

- Eyes are opened.

- Shame is now a part of human existence.

- Adam and Eve attempt to cover their shame.

- God enters the garden.

- Adam and Eve hide in their shame.

What strikes you as interesting regarding this order of events? Do you ever see this order played out in your own life to some degree?

_____

_____

When the Lord God enters the garden, to whom does He call out?

_____

_____

Before confessing, what does Adam say and ultimately do?

_____

_____

It is simple to see that Adam immediately passes the blame to Eve, but as he implicates her, **Accountability** there is a subtle statement. Adam says, "The woman whom <u>You</u> gave to be with me . . ." (Gen. 3:12). Adam did what so many of us do, he blamed God for giving him a circumstance that led to his failure. Take notice that Eve gave the fruit to Adam, but the choice to be disobedient was his and his alone.

After Adam confesses, God questions Eve. Before Eve confesses by saying, "I ate," what does she tell God?

_____

_____

Isn't it interesting that she claimed to have been deceived? She knew the command God had given. That is to say, she knew the truth. Cognitive Atlas defines deception as "acts to propagate beliefs that are not true, or not the whole truth. . . ."[3] Eve knew God's command and chose disobedience.

As discussed earlier, the Edenic covenant was broken and could no longer be observed. For the Lord God to have a relationship with His creation, it was necessary to create another, updated covenant. In the Adamic covenant, the Lord God addressed the consequences for sin and the means of salvation. Let's take a look at the Lord God resetting the path for human history.

Genesis 3:14-21

[14] The LORD God said to the serpent, "Because you have done this, Cursed are you more than all cattle, And more than every beast of the field. On your belly you will go, And dust you will eat All the days of your life;

[15] And I will put enmity between you and the woman, And between your seed and her seed; He shall bruise you on the head, And you shall bruise him on the heel." [16] To the woman He said, "I will greatly multiply Your pain in childbirth, In pain you will bring forth children, Yet your desire will be for your husband, And he will rule over you." [17] Then to Adam He said, "Because you have listened to the voice of your wife, and have eaten from the tree about which I commanded you, saying, 'You shall not eat from it'; Cursed is the ground because of you; In toil you will eat of it All the days of your life. [18] "Both thorns and thistles it shall grow for you; And you will eat the plants

of the field; [19]*By the sweat of your face You will eat bread, Till you return to the ground, Because from it you were taken; For you are dust, And to dust you shall return."* [20]*Now the man called his wife's name Eve, because she was the mother of all the living.* [21]*The* LORD *God made garments of skin for Adam and his wife, and clothed them.*

Who and what was cursed? Were Adam and Eve cursed?

_____

_____

The fact that Adam and Eve were only disciplined should be taken in a way to help us understand the special place that we hold in the heart of God the Father. The first few curses are leveled against the serpent. God then skips over Adam and Eve in terms of curses and, instead, curses the ground. The cursed ground is one of the means by which Adam and Eve are disciplined. The cursed ground is the exact opposite of what they were used to while living in the garden. No longer would their labor be simple and consistently fruitful.

Serpent and Satan

Understanding the serpent can be a bit problematic. A few questions may come to mind:

- Is the serpent actually Satan posing as a serpent? Or was the serpent possessed by Satan? Or was the serpent just a serpent acting under the influence of Satan's evil presence?

- If the serpent is Satan, and Satan is in actuality a fallen angel, why did God curse serpents that are actually serpents?

- If the serpent was possessed by Satan, was he cursed because he was a willing participant or was he an innocent bystander that became a casualty?

Below are some Scriptures provided to facilitate prayerful consideration and discussion. After each Scripture, write down what is revealed about Satan and his abilities to assume or possess other forms and to attack or provoke mankind.

Revelation 12:9

_____

_____

Revelation 20:2

_____

_____

2 Corinthians 11:14

_____

_____

At this point you may be arriving at the conclusion that Satan disguised himself as a serpent. Certainly, this is a fair conclusion. Before you make any conclusive decisions, examine the next three Scriptures:

Genesis 3:1

_____

_____

1 Peter 5:8

_____

_____

Matthew 16:13-23

_____

_____

_____

Let's view the situation with Peter and Jesus and let that illuminate our understanding of the serpent. Jesus rebuked Peter and in His rebuke, He called Peter "Satan." This was not a situation where Peter was transported out of the moment and Satan appeared as Peter and stood in Peter's place. Instead, Jesus rebuked Peter, calling him Satan, and thus, revealing Satan's presence in him. Peter wasn't merely acting on Satan's behalf. That said, physically, he was still Peter. It comes down to a matter of physical state versus functional state.

To help you understand physical and functional a little better let me share this explanation my friend Andrew offered via email to explain the difference in physical creation and functional creation: "Physical creation is when, for instance, a building is erected. Functional creation is when, for instance, that building is assigned a task—say, being a restaurant. When is a building a restaurant? Not when it is physically built, but when it is functioning as one—when money is exchanged for food."[4]

Peter was always Peter in his physical state. For a brief moment, he was functioning as Satan. Peter placed his focus on worldly things, and thus allowed Satan in, and that is why Peter got rebuked. He was functioning as Satan, allowing him to be actively present.

Genesis 3:1 reveals that God created the serpent and the serpent was crafty or clever. Just as

The Adamic Covenant

Peter was physically standing before Jesus, the serpent that Adam and Eve encountered was physically a serpent. Functionally, the serpent was Satan, and not just a naughty snake. When Eve spoke to the serpent, she was speaking to Satan. How did that happen? There are two possible interpretations. 1. Satan transformed himself from being a fallen angel in appearance to being a serpent in appearance. 2. Satan possessed the serpent. As far as the covenant understanding is concerned, either view is acceptable and both views are reasonably supported by Scripture. Because of Genesis 3:15, which we will study shortly, a third and common interpretation will not work. This interpretation states that the serpent was merely influenced by Satan.

Just as Jesus called out and revealed Satan while rebuking Peter, God not only curses the serpent, He curses Satan. God cursed the physical state of the serpent, making it crawl on its belly and eat dust all the days of its life. We can see that God judged the serpent to be culpable and not just an innocent victim. The physical serpent couldn't get away with saying, "The Devil made me do it." We also know that God put enmity (hatred and warfare) between the serpent and the woman, and between the seed of the serpent and the seed of the woman. For our purposes, the question that matters most is, to whom do these seeds refer?

Look at the following Scriptures and write down what they reveal to you about the seed of woman and the seed of the serpent?

Galatians 3:16

_____

_____

Matthew 23:29-34   7:16

_____

_____

1 John 3:8-10 /

_____

_____

_____

Matthew 13:37-39

_____

_____

_____

John 8:44-47

_____

_____

_____

Genesis 3:15 is the central point around which the Adamic covenant revolves. It is known as the "protoevangelium." (I promise, no more big words.) Here, God curses the functional state of the serpent, Satan, "He shall bruise you on the head and you shall bruise him on the heel?"

Read the following verses and summarize how you see the head and the heel being bruised.

Hebrews 2:14

_____

_____

Luke 10:17-19

_____

_____

_____

Romans 16:20

_____

_____

Colossians 2:13-15

_____

_____

_____

Praise God, Who is merciful! No sooner does humanity fall into sin than God reveals a path to redemption. This is not only a declaration of war upon Satan, who is functioning under the cover of the serpent, but it is the covenant promise of victory. The bruising of the heel is the promise that Jesus would one day suffer and die, but the bruising of the head is the promise that Jesus would rise victorious over the grave.

What do the verses above reveal about Satan's power vs. Jesus' power concerning death?

_____

_____

_____

The Adamic Covenant

Take a moment and reflect on relationships you have, both inside and outside of the Christian faith. It might be easy to see how Satan can use non-Christians to influence you, but perhaps you should look more closely at your Christian relationships. Genesis 3:1 clearly shows the serpent to be God's creation. Also, Peter was one of Jesus' three closest companions. Satan is a deceiver. Who better to deceive than a trusted source? Don't get me wrong, I don't want you calling all your Christian friends "Satan," but it is important to recognize words that are contrary to God's Word.

How do you see the functional presence of Satan from time to time in your relationships?

_____

_____

_____

Can you think back and recall a time when you spoke words contrary to the Word of God? In that moment, how were you functioning?

_____

_____

_____

Submission is NOT Subservience

After God addresses the serpent/Satan, who was the instigator of sin, He moves on to address Eve. Many women may want to argue that the pain of childbirth is a curse, but God doesn't actually curse Adam or Eve. Instead, He announces the consequences for their disobedience. I'll let the women in the study speak for the pains of childbirth and what that is all about. Not only is childbirth immensely painful, but child bearing is no picnic either when you consider nausea, vomiting, heartburn, and the plethora of other symptoms accompanying the nine months of pregnancy. With Eve being "the mother of all the living" (Gen. 3:20), she certainly suffered time and again. Not only does she (and all women to follow) bear the consequence of greatly multiplied pain in childbirth, she is given one other consequence. God states, "Yet your desire will be for your husband, and he will rule over you" (Gen. 3:16).

In modern society, this phrase is greatly debated. When Eve took the lead at the tree of knowledge of good and evil, she led her husband into sin. Make no bones about it, he was a willing participant, but Eve took the lead. Therefore, not only was Eve first to enter into sin, she led her husband to do the same thing. Let it be noted that prior to the fall, Adam and Eve were in perfect unity. Sadly, the resulting disunity, as a consequence of sin, necessitated God commanding her to submit to her husband. This was not really anything new as Adam was first in humanity, he was the head of the family before and after the fall.

This command by the Lord God is not to be taken lightly. That said, there are many who will question this one line from verse 16. There are so many ways to argue against the command by asking, "Yeah, but what if . . . ?" or "Did God just mean this for Adam and Eve, but it doesn't continue to apply?" or "Wasn't this command written for a different time and different culture?" While an open and honest exchange of ideas is healthy, arguing will accomplish little. Instead of arguing, perhaps we can pour into the command more deeply and discover a greater truth. Looking further into the command, we can see the promise God gave to Eve as He cursed the serpent. You see, it would be her seed—that is the seed of a woman—which would bring forth the Lord Jesus. Though she was first to enter sin, Jesus, born of a virgin, would be the final sacrifice and the path to redemption. See 1 Timothy 2:15.

It should also be noted at this time that by stating ". . . he will rule over you," God did not intend this to be treated as a master and slave relationship, as we know it. Woman was created as a helpmate. A man should absolutely honor the role of his wife as a helpmate and seek her input, as this was the God-ordained intention of the marriage relationship. We are often quick to quote Ephesians 5:22 regarding wives submitting to their husbands. Let's not forget, however, the preceding verse, "and be subject to one another in the fear of the Lord" (Eph. 5:21). Ultimately, both husband and wife should be submitting to God first and foremost. They should listen to and honor one another. In decision making, when the husband has the better option, the couple goes that way. When the wife has the better option, the couple goes that way. It is when a consensus cannot be reached, as husband and wife submit to God, that the man is to take the position as the ruling authority and be responsible for the decision. Furthermore, it is the man's responsibility to lead his wife into prayerful relationship with God the Father, and he does so by personally submitting himself to God. That said, none of this should exclude compromise and discussion. When two options are on the table of equal or nearly equal value, you'll likely find that submitting to God will reveal the best of both options and a compromise will reveal a third and best option. God gave us mouths for the purpose of communication, not arguing, and certainly not for lording over one another.

Take a few minutes to write down and/or discuss as a group your thoughts regarding the consequences received by Eve. When arguing against commands given by the Lord God, in order to justify our own actions/desires, which character in this story are we most closely emulating?

_____

_____

_____

_____

The Adamic Covenant

When compared to Eve and the serpent, it seems as though the discipline Adam received was reduced. His consequence was one of toil, and seeing futility in his labors. There would be no rest for his toils. The serpent told Eve (and as Adam was standing there, he must have heard also), "you surely will not die" (v. 4). Adam and Eve ate of the fruit and their physical bodies carried on to see another day, but what promise does God give Adam (and Eve) in His corrective actions? See Romans 6:23.

_____

_____

_____

God told Adam, "For you are dust, and to dust you shall return" (v. 19). Though death was not a part of God's intended plan, it was a consequence of sin. The wages of sin is death, and thus death became the ransom that would be paid to free us from sin.

Read Genesis 3:18. Write down the ways in which you see the ground being cursed.

_____

_____

_____

Read Matthew 27:29; John 19:2; Mark 15:17. God chose not to curse Adam or Eve. Who bore the curse of the ground, a curse that was rightfully Adam and Eve's?

_____

_____

The First Sacrifice

Once again, see Romans 6:23. The garments Adam and Eve fashioned out of fig leaves were in no way a lasting solution. What did God have to do in order to create garments for Adam and his wife to clothe them and cover their shame with a lasting solution?

_____

_____

This was the first animal sacrificed in the history of the world. The sacrifice was not used to feed Adam or Eve. God did not use the sacrifice as an offering unto Himself. Instead, this sacrifice was used to cover the newly chosen sin of Adam and Eve.

I am humbled as I struggle to imagine God preparing the garments for Adam and Eve. I keep wondering what God was experiencing as He sacrificed the first animal in history, knowing the sacrifice was sufficient to cover their newfound shame, but not enough to cover the sins of humanity. All the while, He knew the lasting solution would be the act of putting His own child to death on a cross. Praise God! Our merciful Father did not spare His own son, to save sinners such as ourselves.

Closing Reflections

What do God's corrective actions reveal about how He views humanity?

How do God's corrective actions preserve humanity's relationship with Him?

How would you describe your responsibilities toward God's Word?

Join the Conversation on:

Facebook: facebook.com/Thecovenantschristandyou Like and Post your thoughts on God's covenant with Adam and Eve.

or

Twitter: @CovChristU Tweet your thoughts on God's covenant with Adam and Eve.

Engaging Others:

Pray. Ask God to begin stirring in the lives of those in your sphere of influence. One of the greatest tools we have for engagement is prayer. Be diligent in your prayer. Ask God to reveal to you people whose hearts are going to be receptive to His revelation through covenant. God knows your heart, so there's no need for a hashtag.

Chapter 3
The Noahic Covenant

As for you, be fruitful and multiply; Populate the earth abundantly and multiply in it.

—Genesis 9:7

It's the story we've all heard so many times since we were children. I must admit, growing up, I was a huge fan of the story of Noah and the Ark. In fact, I could even tell you his first and last names: Noah Zark. I was absolutely certain, but my mom eventually set me straight on the facts. . . well. . . she cleared up that last name issue anyway.

Pre-adolescent language issue aside, it's a great story, with a rich oral story-telling tradition. It's a story with so much to offer, a story of a good man who listens to God and builds a boat to save himself, his family, and two of every kind of animal. God wipes away all the bad people and makes a promise not to flood the whole earth again. Finally, He makes a rainbow to be a reminder of His promise. The story we hear as kids has all the great elements of story-telling; a protagonist, antagonists, climax, resolution and a happily-ever-after at the very end. What kid doesn't love this story?

It is a story that brings comfort when the heavy rains fall. We can be certain that there will be a place to find dry ground, because God made a promise. However, so much of the story we know from our youth gets embellished and oversimplified. It becomes quick and easy fodder for those who are prone to questioning its validity and its application.

In this study, we're going to be looking at Genesis, Chapters 6–9. Our main focus is chapter **Clarification** 9. I would recommend reading all 4 chapters, but that may need to happen outside of group time.

The Noahic Covenant

We'll typically start with Scripture, but this time, let's start with a few "true or false" statements to clear up possible misconceptions.

True or False: There is a Biblical account stating, specifically, the length of time that it took Noah to build the ark.

Many believe that it took 120 years because of Genesis 6:3. ". . . nevertheless his days shall be one hundred and twenty years." Genesis 5:32 states, "Noah was five hundred years old, and Noah became the father of Shem, Ham, and Japheth." Additionally, Genesis states, "Now Noah was six hundred years old when the flood of water came upon the earth." (Gen. 7:6) This means God would have spoken to Noah when he was 480 years of age and 20 years before he had his three sons, meaning Noah spent several years working on the ark all by himself. You can also read about building boats from wood and what conditions are optimal for the age of the cut wood and then take into account an extremely different pre-flood climate and ultimately know, you just don't know anything for certain.

True or False: There is a Biblical account of Noah having a discussion with God and asking questions regarding His command.

It seems logical to assume there was an exchange where Noah presented questions, but you won't find a record of it in the Bible.

True or False: There is a Biblical account of Noah being ridiculed by others as he built the ark.

It is often assumed that he was ridiculed and this assumption certainly has Biblical backing when one considers the Adamic covenant, where God tells the serpent, "And I will put enmity between you and the woman . . ." (Gen. 3:15). Noah was a descendant from the holy line of Seth (the seed of the woman). While we can speculate that he was ridiculed, the Bible does not specifically state this.

For a story that covers four chapters in the Bible, it may seem to some that there is surprisingly little detail. You may be inclined to ask all sorts of questions and truly want the answers. Please understand, different people have vastly different informational desires. Let me give you an example:

I can learn my friends, Joe and Sally, had their 8 lb 11 oz baby. I might even know that the baby was a little girl named Suzy. Additionally, I probably know Sally and Suzy are doing well and Joe is really tired. Thinking that is good information, I bring it to my wife. I then realize all the deficits in my story. For instance, the questions I should have asked Joe are: When is Sally's mom coming to town to help with the baby? How long was she in labor? Where is their other daughter, Regina, staying while Sally and Suzy are in the hospital? Which room is Sally in? The questions go on and on. I now know, if my friend calls about a newborn baby, it's best to hand the phone off to my wife and tell her to pounce.

This said, and all joking aside, regardless of our informational desires, God is going to give us what we need to know in order to understand what we need to learn. So, using just the Biblical facts, let's take a look at what God reveals to us in Genesis regarding Noah and the ark.

Read Genesis 6:5-7,11-12. What reason does God give for sending the flood?

Background
and
Covenant

_____

_____

_____

Read Genesis 6:10, 18; Genesis 7:13. How many people were on the ark?

_____

_____

Read Genesis 7:1-4,11 and Genesis 8:14-16. Most people understand that Noah and his family were on the ark during a storm that lasted 40 days and 40 nights, and then they add in the releasing of the raven and dove, to come to a figure of around 55-60 days. However, what does this tell you regarding the length of time Noah and his family were on the ark?

_____

_____

(Genesis 8:1-13 has the days broken down a little more thoroughly, but the calculations become a bit dizzying.)

The Noahic covenant is first mentioned in Genesis 6:18, however, the details of the covenant are not revealed until Genesis 9. It is the first time God uses the term "covenant." Let's take a look at what the covenant states.

Genesis 9:1-17

¹*And God blessed Noah and his sons and said to them, "Be fruitful and multiply, and fill the earth.* ²*"The fear of you and the terror of you will be on every beast of the earth and on every bird of the sky; with everything that creeps on the ground, and all the fish of the sea, into your hand they are given.* ³*"Every moving thing that is alive shall be food for you; I give all to you, as I gave the green plant.* ⁴*"Only you shall not eat flesh with its life, that is, its blood.* ⁵*"Surely I will require your lifeblood; from every beast I*

41

The Noahic Covenant

will require it. And from every man, from every man's brother I will require the life of man. [6]"Whoever sheds man's blood, By man his blood shall be shed, For in the image of God He made man. [7]"As for you, be fruitful and multiply; Populate the earth abundantly and multiply in it." [8]Then God spoke to Noah and to his sons with him, saying, [9]"Now behold, I Myself do establish My covenant with you, and with your descendants after you; [10]and with every living creature that is with you, the birds, the cattle, and every beast of the earth with you; of all that comes out of the ark, even every beast of the earth. [11]"I establish My covenant with you; and all flesh shall never again be cut off by the water of the flood, neither shall there again be a flood to destroy the earth." [12]God said, "This is the sign of the covenant which I am making between Me and you and every living creature that is with you, for all successive generations; [13]I set My bow in the cloud, and it shall be for a sign of a covenant between Me and the earth. [14]"It shall come about, when I bring a cloud over the earth, that the bow will be seen in the cloud, [15]and I will remember My covenant, which is between Me and you and every living creature of all flesh; and never again shall the water become a flood to destroy all flesh. [16]"When the bow is in the cloud, then I will look upon it, to remember the everlasting covenant between God and every living creature of all flesh that is on the earth." [17]And God said to Noah, "This is the sign of the covenant which I have established between Me and all flesh that is on the earth."

What does the Bible say God does first for Noah and his sons? What command does He give them? (v.1)

_____

_____

_____

This is the second account of God stating this command to be fruitful and multiply, the first being on the sixth day of creation. It stands to reason that God should give such a command at this time as it is a time of new beginnings

Blood in the Covenant
After God gives Noah and his sons the command, a pivotal moment occurs in the dietary life of humankind. God tells them, "Every moving thing that is alive shall be food for you; I give all to you, as I gave the green plant." Following this life-altering statement, God lays out one limitation. He says, "Only you shall not eat flesh with its life, that is, its blood." This statement shows that the animal must be killed and the blood let out. There should be no question as to whether or not any life is still in the animal before consuming it.

This clarification of the state of the flesh to be consumed serves two purposes. The first purpose served is the prevention of cruelty. Consider the destination to which the path of animal cruelty leads. As a person becomes tolerant of the suffering of animals and inflicting of pain, he/she becomes desensitized. From there it is a small step into cruelty to our fellow humans. This is a path our heavenly Father does not desire for us.

The second purpose is equally intriguing. Research has shown blood— animal or human— to have no nutritional value for people. It contains iron and negligible amounts of protein. Oddly though, the human body does not absorb those proteins or iron and voids itself of the blood as quickly as possible. I'll spare you the less pleasant details.

The command also restricts a person who is offering an animal sacrifice from drinking the blood. It may seem odd that so much time is being spent on this particular command, but we're going to explore the implications of the commands regarding animal consumption and blood consumption just a bit more. So let's discuss a few questions.

Read Genesis 9:6 and Genesis 1:27. What is common between these two verses?

_____

_____

_____

Read James 1:18. How does God view animals in contrast to humans?

_____

_____

_____

Please don't allow this to spiral downward into a time of pitting science against the Bible, but how is God's view of animals and humans different from what we commonly hear in science classes regarding the classification of species?

_____

_____

_____

As God created man in His own image, He established the sanctity of human life. He placed His human creation above the rest of creation. Science classes, for all the good that comes out of them, tend to philosophically dehumanize humans. In terms of classification of various species, we fall into the animal kingdom, as we just don't have much of anything in common with plants. The problem with this is not one of scientific methodology, but is instead a philosophical issue. If we allow ourselves to accept that we are animals and nothing more, we fail to accept our God-ordained place in creation and subsequently devalue our humanity, followed by acceptance of animalistic behavior.

Animal sacrifice by humans is recorded as early as Abel. It was clearly a part of the culture, serving as an offering to God. When you consider humanity's place in God's creation, how does that affect the value of one man's sacrifice on the cross (Jesus) versus men sacrificing animals?

_____

_____

_____

Jesus' death on the cross was a complete and final atonement for all of humanity. It put an end to the value of all animal sacrifices. If we equate humans with all other animals, it devalues Christ's act upon the cross and reduces Him to just another animal. God does not see humanity in this way.

Read John 6:54. We read in the various accounts of the last supper that Jesus passed the cup as a symbol of His blood being poured out for us. As stated earlier, blood has no nutritional qualities and therefore has no life-sustaining qualities. In John 6:54, what do we learn about the blood of Jesus?

_____

_____

_____

Read Genesis 9:6-7. How do verses 6 and 7 work together in communicating God's expectations regarding life? Are there consequences for working against this command?

_____

_____

_____

Read Matthew 28:19-20 and Genesis 1:27-28. Jesus' final command to His disciples is one of multiplication, much like God's first command to mankind. In choosing Noah, God chose a righteous man. What do you think was supposed to multiply alongside the multiplication of human beings?

_____

_____

_____

Following the commands, God presents His covenant through a promise to Noah, his sons, all of his descendants, and every living creature. It is the part of the story with which we are most familiar. What is that promise? What does He create as a reminder of His promise?

_____

_____

_____

Has God broken His covenant? Is there anything we humans can do to cause Him to break the covenant?

_____

_____

The only time covenants have been broken is through an act of mankind. The Noahic covenant is called an unconditional covenant. God did not promise He would not flood the earth just so long as . . . . He simply promised not to flood the entire earth again. Human beings have no responsibility toward this covenant any longer.

Summarize the following verses:

Genesis 6:9

_____

_____

_____

Genesis 8:21

_____

_____

_____

Why Noah?

The Noahic Covenant

Mark 10:18

_____

_____

_____

Romans 3:23

_____

_____

_____

Was Noah a perfect man in the sense that he was without sin?

_____

_____

_____

So . . . Why Noah? We could certainly make an argument right now regarding Noah's fleshly lineage, as he was a descendant in the holy line of Seth; however, that may be selling Noah just a little bit short. God chose Noah for a reason. In Genesis 6:9, we learn Noah was a righteous man, and the verse states, "Noah walked with God."

Read Genesis 6:22; Genesis 8:18-20. What do these verses reveal about Noah that exemplifies his righteousness and how he walked with God?

_____

_____

_____

Noah's response to God's command was obedience. His first act upon leaving the ark was in no way self-serving. While most people would be very goal oriented, realizing a need to establish a permanent home, Noah chose to serve God. God's provision was apparent to Noah. He knew he had plenty of shelter in the ark and a more permanent solution could wait until he served his Lord. Noah's righteousness was not an indication of a perfect and sinless life; rather it was an indication of his desire to be a godly man, a man with a desire to be with his Creator.

Having selected Noah as the man to carry out the plan, could God have established His covenant with Noah had he chosen disobedience? The answer is clearly "no." What does this tell you about your response to God's will being revealed in your life?

_____

_____

_____

The covenant in Eden established how to be obedient. The covenant with Adam established what happens when we are disobedient. And finally, God's covenant with Noah reveals what happens when we are obedient.

Closing Reflections

What does God reveal about humanity's special place in His creation?

Read Genesis 8:20-22. As you read God's response to Noah's faithful act of offering burnt offerings, what is revealed to you about God and who He is?

_____

Join the Conversation on:

Facebook: facebook.com/Thecovenantschristandyou Like and Post your thoughts on God's covenant with Noah

or

Twitter: @CovChristU Tweet your thoughts on God's covenant with Noah

Engaging Others:

Small groups and Sunday School: Each member Tweet it, Post it, Pin it, or Instagram a picture of the person sitting closest to you in your discussion of *The Covenants, Christ, and You.* Tweet it to @CovChristU or Tag the Facebook page.

The Noahic Covenant

Individuals and Discipleship: Selfie-Time! Tweet it, Post it, Pin it, or Instagram a selfie of you or both of you with your copy of *The Covenants, Christ, and You*. Tweet it to @CovChristU or Tag the Facebook page.

Suggested Hashtags
#Discipleship #ChristFollower #BibleStudy #SmallGroup #Evangelism #Relevant #Jesus
If you're not on social media, with whom can you share this study?

Keep praying for those in your sphere of influence that the Holy Spirit would stir in their hearts and create a thirst for God to reveal Himself in mighty ways in their lives.

Chapter 4

The Abrahamic Covenant

Then he believed in the Lord; and He reckoned it to him as righteousness.

—Genesis 15:6

I find the calls of Noah and Abram (Abraham) to be somewhat peculiar in their contrast. When God called Noah to build the ark, He stated very clearly that a covenant would be established. However, outside of saving Noah, his family, and two of every kind of animal, God revealed none of the covenant details. Perhaps the understanding of eminent death was enough for Noah to be obedient, and preservation of life mattered more than any other details beyond that.

Abram's call is quite different. Abram receives many details, but the one thing he doesn't know is that a covenant is to be established. Instead, God gives him a charge and lets Abram know how he will be blessed. Abram very well may realize he is entering a covenant, but from our standpoint, we don't actually see God use that term. Additionally, what we see first is an initial charge, but God reveals more charges for Abram and more about the overall covenant over a period greater than 25 years.

Genesis 12:1-3

¹*Now the LORD said to Abram, "Go forth from your country, And from your relatives And from your father's house, To the land which I will show you; ²And I will make you a great nation, And I will bless you, And make your name great; And so you shall be a blessing; ³And I will bless those who bless you, And the one who curses you I will curse. And in you all the families of the earth will be blessed."*

The Abrahamic Covenant

In the first verse, God charges Abram. What is that charge?

_____

_____

_____

Look closely at Genesis 12:1-3. Name six things God promises Abram. (These are the foundational promises of the covenant God would establish with Abram as a result of Abram's obedience.)

1.

2.

3.

4.

5.

6.

Faithful and Available

Read Genesis 12:4-9. After God shows Abram the land which He would give to Abram's descendants, Abram builds an altar at the oak of Moreh. While in the land of Canaan, Abram and his family are in enemy territory. This isn't Abram's land. Yet, as a bold statement of his faith in the Word of God, Abram builds an altar. Then we see Abram proceed to an area between Bethel and Ai, and there he pitches his tent and builds another altar, calling upon the name of the Lord.

What does this reveal to you about Abram that he would build altars in these temporary locations?

_____

_____

_____

Abram was not just a man of faith, he was faithful, meaning that he didn't just accept God's word for himself, he acted upon God's word. He took his faith with him everywhere he went. He practiced his faith and brought his family, and those in his charge, into his faith. He habitually did what was pleasing to God. Worship was a natural state for Abram.

It should be noted at this time that the journey to Canaan was a continuation of the journey Abram began with his father, Terah, in Genesis 11. Though we don't actually see God tell Abram where to go, Canaan isn't just a random choice. We don't know why Terah had chosen to travel that way. Could it have been a call from God? Was it a place Terah just always wanted to travel? We don't know, but we do know that it apparently played into God's plan for Abram.

In Genesis 12 and 13, we see God promise to give the land to Abram's descendants. That probably sounds a bit odd to us as we consider that Abram was 75 years old and had no children of his own. However, in the culture of the day, anyone born in Abram's household could have been considered a descendant. If you take the time to read from Genesis 12–Genesis 25, you will see some land was given to Abram and even see that he purchased some land, however, it should not escape your attention that Abram lived a largely nomadic lifestyle. At the age of 99 he still lived in a tent. In other words, Abram and his family were very mobile. Furthermore, Abram never served as a ruler over the land of Canaan.

So often, we become settled in our lives as we call our material possessions, and especially our homes, a blessing. God won't necessarily call everyone to be mobile as He called Abram. Some, He may call to be steadfast. What is important, is your willingness to submit and let God make the call, rather than choosing something that just seems comfortable.

Take time to discuss as a group, or write down your thoughts about, how our possessions and our attitudes toward them, for better or worse, affect our mobility in response to God's call.

_____

_____

_____

In His initial charge to Abram, God tells Abram, "I will bless you." and "I will make your name great." All other promises to Abram really affect Abram's descendants, and the world at large, far more than they affect him. Who do you believe Abram was most interested in pleasing, himself or his Lord God?

_____

_____

Read Exodus 3:6; Matthew 22:32; Acts 3:13. How did God fulfill His promise to make Abram's name great?

_____

_____

_____

The Abrahamic Covenant

Reckoning
Righteousness
Although we don't have a specific timeline for all the events of Abram's life, we can definitely see a chronological order. Prior to chapter 15, when the covenant is actually established, Abram and his men travel into harm's way in order to rescue his nephew Lot, Lot's family, and the people and goods of the kingdom of Sodom. He has an encounter with the king of Sodom who offers Abram all the goods he recovered. Abram refuses the goods as He had already promised God not to take anything from Sodom, for he did not want this wicked king to have any claim on his prosperity. We pick up in chapter 15 where it begins "After these things . . . ." As stated earlier, we don't know an actual timeline, but we know it happened sometime in the first ten years Abram and his family were living in the land of Canaan.

Genesis 15

[1]*After these things the word of the LORD came to Abram in a vision, saying, "Do not fear, Abram, I am a shield to you; Your reward shall be very great."* [2]*Abram said, "O Lord GOD, what will You give me, since I am childless, and the heir of my house is Eliezer of Damascus?"* [3]*And Abram said, "Since You have given no offspring to me, one born in my house is my heir."* [4]*Then behold, the word of the LORD came to him, saying, "This man will not be your heir; but one who will come forth from your own body, he shall be your heir."* [5]*And He took him outside and said, "Now look toward the heavens, and count the stars, if you are able to count them." And He said to him, "So shall your descendants be."* [6]*Then he believed in the LORD; and He reckoned it to him as righteousness.* [7]*And He said to him, "I am the LORD who brought you out of Ur of the Chaldeans, to give you this land to possess it."* [8]*He said, "O Lord GOD, how may I know that I will possess it?"* [9]*So He said to him, "Bring Me a three year old heifer, and a three year old female goat, and a three year old ram, and a turtledove, and a young pigeon."* [10]*Then he brought all these to Him and cut them in two, and laid each half opposite the other; but he did not cut the birds.* [11]*The birds of prey came down upon the carcasses, and Abram drove them away.* [12]*Now when the sun was going down, a deep sleep fell upon Abram; and behold, terror and great darkness fell upon him.* [13]*God said to Abram, "Know for certain that your descendants will be strangers in a land that is not theirs, where they will be enslaved and oppressed four hundred years.* [14]*"But I will also judge the nation whom they will serve, and afterward they will come out with many possessions.* [15]*"As for you, you shall go to your fathers in peace; you will be buried at a good old age.* [16]*"Then in the fourth generation they will return here, for the iniquity of the Amorite is not yet complete."* [17]*It came about when the sun had set, that it was very dark, and behold, there appeared a smoking oven and a flaming torch which passed between these pieces.* [18]*On that day the LORD made a covenant with Abram, saying, "To your descendants I have given this land, From the river of Egypt as far as the great river, the river Euphrates:* [19]*the Kenite and the Kenizzite and the Kadmonite* [20]*and the Hittite and the Perizzite and the Rephaim* [21]*and the Amorite and the Canaanite and the Girgashite and the Jebusite."*

God states, "Do not fear, Abram. I am a shield to you . . . ." How does this change the dynamic of Abram's relationship with The Lord God?

_____

_____

_____

Read the following verses and write down what they reveal about God being a shield.

Psalms 28:7

_____

_____

Psalms 18:2

_____

_____

Psalms 84:11

_____

_____

Proverbs 30:5

_____

_____

How would your relationship with God change, if you considered Him a shield to you?

_____

_____

_____

God does not simply restate the covenant from chapter 12 and establish it in chapter 15. He seems to do much more. List the things you see as differences between the initial charge and what you see established in the covenant. Does the blessing seem smaller or greater than God's initial promise? What does this reveal about God the Father?

_____

_____

_____

_____

The Abrahamic Covenant

God established that the land would be given to Abram's fleshly descendants. Instead of numbering Abram's descendants by the dust of the earth, He used the stars as His reference. God established geographical boundaries for the land that would be possessed by Abram's descendants. The blessings are greater. God doesn't go back on His promises, but He is moved by obedience and is ready to bless us in abundance when we faithfully carry out His will.

The covenant ceremony was often performed between two people. The act of passing through the split halves of the carcasses was a way of saying, "If I break this covenant, so should I experience this same fate." We see the smoking oven and flaming torch, no doubt symbolic of The Lord God, pass between the split halves. We do not, however, see Abram pass between the split halves. Why was Abram exempt from this part of the ceremony?

_____

_____

_____

Consider for a moment, the observance of the Lord's Supper. Can you see a parallel between the covenant ceremony observed between God and Abram, and the covenant ceremony over which Jesus presided in the upper room? Read 1 Corinthians 11:23-24.

_____

_____

_____

I cannot think of a communion service where I saw bread literally being broken that it was not broken in half or close to it. That is to say, I've never seen a ceremonial first break that might be considered 95% and 5%. It is usually very close to 50/50. As I consider Jesus on the cross, I envision a high degree of visual symmetry with his outstretched arms. In breaking the bread, Jesus symbolically split His body in half. As we partake in the loaf and the cup, we symbolically pass through the split halves.

Broken Identity   As the Bible takes us into Chapter 16, we see Sarai give her maid Hagar to her husband so that she could bear him a child, as Sarai was barren. Because we don't know the exact timeline for the events of chapter 15, we don't know with any certainty how long Abram and Sarai tried to conceive prior to this decision. What we do know is that this particular event occurred 10 years after they began living in Canaan.

Sarai is often vilified for her decision to give Hagar to her husband, and Abram tends to receive a degree of castigation for receiving Hagar. So often we talk about how they didn't trust God and that they acted in haste. I don't want to refute that, but I'd like to point out two observations, which lead to a couple of important ideas that we tend to overlook. First, and this is no excuse, but what they did fell within the cultural norms and customs. By giving Hagar to her husband and their subsequently having a child, Sarai would obtain a child according to the prevalent practice of the day. Instead of merely focusing on the sinfulness of the action, it may be more beneficial to focus some attention on the brokenness of Sarai as she crumbled under her self-perceived inadequacies and gave in to the cultural practice rather than giving in to God. Sarai and Abram gave in to the cultural customs and, therefore, we arrive at our second observation, that being, at no point do we see The Lord God scold them for making that decision. He very well may have as, clearly, this was not the path God intended for Abram and Sarai. However, we don't see it because a reprimand from God isn't the main point. The main point is that God's will isn't bound by our decisions or our understanding of the world, and therefore, He eventually corrects the course.

The lack of a reprimand should not leave you with the impression that God gave Abram and Sarai a free pass based on cultural norms, and therefore, God allows culture to dictate what is and is not sin. In fact, the opposite is true. God determines what is and is not sin. We don't get to continue in sin because it is our cultural norm. Whatever separates us from the love of the Father will do so regardless of the cultural customs we practice. Sometimes, it is cultural norms which provide the final blow in breaking us.

Take a few moments to reflect on a time when, in your brokenness, you gave in to the cultural pressure surrounding you. Or, look at your life and consider what cultural norms are weighing heavily on you and straining your relationship with God. To whom should your brokenness lead you?

_____

_____

_____

At the age of 86, Abram has a son named Ishmael. After Ishmael is born, the Bible jumps 13 years. Because the story of this extraordinarily faithful man continues, we know the Lord God wasn't done with his servant Abram. During this time, we have no record of any interactions between God and Abram. We don't know anything about his nomadic travels or anything else about what Abram did for 13 years. Was this a judgment for Abram's and Sarai's lack of trust? We don't know with absolute certainty, but God's timing is often a mystery to us and it may have seemed so to Abram as well. Nevertheless, when Abram was ready, God pursued him and gave Abram the opportunity to grow even deeper in relationship with his Creator.

Genesis 17

¹*Now when Abram was ninety-nine years old, the LORD appeared to Abram and said to him, "I am God Almighty; Walk before Me, and be blameless. ²"I will establish My covenant between Me and you, And I will multiply you exceedingly." ³Abram fell on his face, and God talked with him, saying, ⁴"As for Me, behold, My covenant is with you, And you will be the father of a multitude of nations. ⁵"No longer shall your name be called Abram, But your name shall be Abraham; For I have made you the father of a multitude of nations. ⁶"I will make you exceedingly fruitful, and I will make nations of you, and kings will come forth from you. ⁷"I will establish My covenant between Me and you and your descendants after you throughout their generations for an everlasting covenant, to be God to you and to your descendants after you. ⁸"I will give to you and to your descendants after you, the land of your sojournings, all the land of Canaan, for an everlasting possession; and I will be their God."*

⁹*God said further to Abraham, "Now as for you, you shall keep My covenant, you and your descendants after you throughout their generations. ¹⁰"This is My covenant, which you shall keep, between Me and you and your descendants after you: every male among you shall be circumcised. ¹¹"And you shall be circumcised in the flesh of your foreskin, and it shall be the sign of the covenant between Me and you. ¹²"And every male among you who is eight days old shall be circumcised throughout your generations, a servant who is born in the house or who is bought with money from any foreigner, who is not of your descendants. ¹³"A servant who is born in your house or who is bought with your money shall surely be circumcised; thus shall My covenant be in your flesh for an everlasting covenant. ¹⁴"But an uncircumcised male who is not circumcised in the flesh of his foreskin, that person shall be cut off from his people; he has broken My covenant."*

¹⁵*Then God said to Abraham, "As for Sarai your wife, you shall not call her name Sarai, but Sarah shall be her name. ¹⁶"I will bless her, and indeed I will give you a son by her. Then I will bless her, and she shall be a mother of nations; kings of peoples will come from her." ¹⁷Then Abraham fell on his face and laughed, and said in his heart, "Will a child be born to a man one hundred years old? And will Sarah, who is ninety years old, bear a child?" ¹⁸And Abraham said to God, "Oh that Ishmael might live before You!" ¹⁹But God said, "No, but Sarah your wife will bear you a son, and you shall call his name Isaac; and I will establish My covenant with him for an everlasting covenant for his descendants after him. ²⁰"As for Ishmael, I have heard you; behold, I will bless him, and will make him fruitful and will multiply him exceedingly. He shall become the father of twelve princes, and I will make him a great nation. ²¹"But My covenant I will establish with Isaac, whom Sarah will bear to you at this season next year." ²²When He finished talking with him, God went up from Abraham.*

²³*Then Abraham took Ishmael his son, and all the servants who were born in his*

house and all who were bought with his money, every male among the men of Abraham's household, and circumcised the flesh of their foreskin in the very same day, as God had said to him. ²⁴Now Abraham was ninety-nine years old when he was circumcised in the flesh of his foreskin. ²⁵And Ishmael his son was thirteen years old when he was circumcised in the flesh of his foreskin. ²⁶In the very same day Abraham was circumcised, and Ishmael his son. ²⁷All the men of his household, who were born in the house or bought with money from a foreigner, were circumcised with him.

In the first verse, God charges Abram a second time. What charge does God give to Abram?

Second Revelation

_____

_____

_____

Read Exodus 3:13-14. In light of this passage from Exodus 3, examine the following three statements from Genesis 17:

I am God Almighty (in Hebrew, *El-Shaddai*).

Walk before Me, and be blameless.

Abram fell on his face.

Take time individually to write down your impressions of this encounter between God and Abram. Place yourself in Abram's sandals. Then, as a small group, discuss your individual impressions.

_____

_____

_____

_____

_____

When we take time to really exam this moment, the weight of these three phrases is overwhelming. To place myself before The Almighty, who just spoke His glorious name, I AM, I can't imagine the depths of my inadequacies.

This is the first time God calls Himself "Almighty." The last time they spoke, God described Himself as a "shield." That Abram would fall to his face indicates that God revealed Himself in a

The Abrahamic Covenant

much more glorious and profound way. We don't see Abram have this response to God before this moment. Humble and obedient, yes, but not physically face down on the ground. God's display of power and might must have been magnificent. In the book of Genesis, there is no detailed description of what Abraham saw. We can't say for certain that he saw the same thing, but John has a very similar reaction in the first chapter of Revelation when he encounters Jesus, the man who did walk blameless, in His glorified body, proclaiming the name, Almighty.

Read Revelation 1:8,12-18. To develop your sense of what John saw, and what Abraham may have seen, write down a list of descriptors John provides.

_____

_____

_____

_____

_____

_____

_____

_____

_____

In the second verse, God states, "I will establish my covenant with you, and multiply you exceedingly." How can this statement be reconciled with the fact that God already established the covenant in chapter fifteen?

_____

_____

_____

In the 17th chapter we find God introducing a new charge for Abram. In fact, he receives a new name, Abraham. The charge is in addition to what God charged in chapter 12. The first charge was to go forth, and the new charge tells Abram to be blameless as he walks before the Lord God Almighty. As we will see very quickly, the covenant expands once again.

How does God describe the covenant with Abraham's descendants? (v. 13)

_____

_____

In the initial charge, God told Abram, "I will make you a great nation" (Gen. 12:2). In chapter 17, God changes his name to Abraham because Abram means _high father_ and God had another plan for Abraham. What reason does God give for naming him Abraham?

_____

_____

God tells Abraham, "Kings will come forth from you." As the father of a multitude of nations, many kings came forth from Abraham's line. Read Isaiah 9:6 and 1 Timothy 1:16-17. What is the connection between the everlasting covenant and the kings which would come forth from Abraham's line?

_____

_____

_____

A Son is Given

In a correction of the course taken 13 years earlier by Abram and Sarai to have a son through Hagar, God reveals one more part of the promise: Sarai (henceforth Sarah) would give birth to a son, and Abraham was to name him Isaac. What does God reveal about His covenant as it relates to Ishmael and Isaac?

_____

_____

_____

That the covenant would be established through Isaac, not Ishmael, is a very important fact when one begins to look at foreign affairs. The nation of Israel tracks its lineage through Isaac, while many Arabs track their lineage through Ishmael. (Some track it through the line of Ham as they became the Canaanites.) The reason this is important is because Muslims understand the covenant as having been established through Ishmael and, therefore, they claim rights to the land of Canaan. As mentioned, some Arabs trace their lineage through the line of Ham and that is why they claim the land of Canaan, as Canaan was Ham's descendent. The feud between the nation of Israel and the Muslim religion traces all the way back to Genesis 17. (See Genesis 16:11-12.)

Much like God putting His bow in the sky as a sign of the Noahic covenant, God revealed to Abraham that he and his descendants would have a sign. What sign was required of Abraham?

_____

Everything I Have . . .

Genesis 22:1-18

[1]*Now it came about after these things, that God tested Abraham, and said to him, "Abraham!" And he said, "Here I am."* [2]*He said, "Take now your son, your only son, whom you love, Isaac, and go to the land of Moriah, and offer him there as a burnt offering on one of the mountains of which I will tell you."* [3]*So Abraham rose early in the morning and saddled his donkey, and took two of his young men with him and Isaac his son; and he split wood for the burnt offering, and arose and went to the place of which God had told him.* [4]*On the third day Abraham raised his eyes and saw the place from a distance.* [5]*Abraham said to his young men, "Stay here with the donkey, and I and the lad will go over there; and we will worship and return to you."* [6]*Abraham took the wood of the burnt offering and laid it on Isaac his son, and he took in his hand the fire and the knife. So the two of them walked on together.* [7]*Isaac spoke to Abraham his father and said, "My father!" And he said, "Here I am, my son." And he said, "Behold, the fire and the wood, but where is the lamb for the burnt offering?"* [8]*Abraham said, "God will provide for Himself the lamb for the burnt offering, my son." So the two of them walked on together.*

[9]*Then they came to the place of which God had told him; and Abraham built the altar there and arranged the wood, and bound his son Isaac and laid him on the altar, on top of the wood.* [10]*Abraham stretched out his hand and took the knife to slay his son.* [11]*But the angel of the LORD called to him from heaven and said, "Abraham, Abraham!" And he said, "Here I am."* [12]*He said, "Do not stretch out your hand against the lad, and do nothing to him; for now I know that you fear God, since you have not withheld your son, your only son, from Me."* [13]*Then Abraham raised his eyes and looked, and behold, behind him a ram caught in the thicket by his horns; and Abraham went and took the ram and offered him up for a burnt offering in the place of his son.* [14]*Abraham called the name of that place The LORD Will Provide, as it is said to this day, "In the mount of the LORD it will be provided."*

[15]*Then the angel of the LORD called to Abraham a second time from heaven,* [16]*and said, "By Myself I have sworn, declares the LORD, because you have done this thing and have not withheld your son, your only son,* [17]*indeed I will greatly bless you, and I will greatly multiply your seed as the stars of the heavens and as the sand which is on the seashore; and your seed shall possess the gate of their enemies.* [18]*"In your seed all the nations of the earth shall be blessed, because you have obeyed My voice."*

In Genesis 22, we see Abraham receive his third and final charge from the Lord God. Read the following verses and write down how Abraham was charged to live a life like Jesus:

John 14:2

_____

_____

John 1:1-2,14

_____

_____

2 Corinthians 5:21

_____

_____

John 3:16

_____

_____

Luke 23:46

_____

_____

The final expansion of the covenant shows Abraham's seed being greatly multiplied, putting together the stars of the heaven and the sand of the seashore. Additionally, God tells Abraham "your seed shall possess the gate of their enemies," and "in your seed all the nations of the earth shall be blessed" (Gen. 22:17-18).

. . . Is Yours

Read 1 Corinthians 15:54-57. Possession of the gates is a reference to victory. How did Abraham's seed possess the gate of their enemies?

_____

_____

_____

The covenant promises reveal that all families will be blessed through Abram and that all nations will be blessed in the seed of Abraham. The blessing was supposed to be upon his descendants.

The Abrahamic Covenant

How do we obtain the inheritance intended for Abraham's descendants? Read Galatians 3:7-9,28-29; Romans 8:15.

_____

_____

_____

Closing Reflections

Abraham placed God at the very center of his life. How does God respond to us when we have placed Him at the center of our lives?

Below, there has been a circle drawn. Imagine this circle is a representation of your life. Place a mark in the place God holds in your life. Keep in mind, there is no sense being dishonest. It is when we get honest with God, and ask Him to change us, that He begins to move in mighty ways in our lives. After you have placed your mark, take time to write down your thoughts about God's place in your life. This only needs to be shared with others if you choose to share with others.

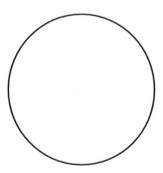

Join the Conversation on:

Facebook: facebook.com/Thecovenantschristandyou Like and Post your thoughts on God's covenant with Abraham

or

Twitter: @CovChristU Tweet your thoughts on God's covenant with Abraham.

Engaging Others:

Tweet it, Post it, Pin it, or Instagram a picture of something that represents what one would find if we could venture into the center of your life. It could simply be a picture of the word written on a piece of paper. Provide a short reflection on your thoughts about the picture. Tweet it to @CovChristU or Tag the Facebook page.

Suggested Hashtags
#Discipleship #ChristFollower #BibleStudy #SmallGroup #Evangelism #Relevant #Jesus

Keep praying for God to stir in the lives of those in your sphere of influence. Begin asking God to not only lay people on your heart, but to begin creating openings to share the message of His covenants. This is easy stuff for extroverts, but if you're an introvert start praying for God to fill you with peace that transcends understanding so you can step forward to share His word.

Chapter 5

The Mosaic Covenant

Then I will take you for My people, and I will be your God;
and you shall know that I am the Lord your God.

—Exodus 6:7

After the covenant with Abraham was established, the book of Genesis traces the lives of his descendants; Isaac, Jacob (who would become Israel by name) and Joseph. The blessing and promise was handed down from generation to generation. And, as God told Abraham, his descendants found themselves in bondage in the land of Egypt. They had become a numerous people, and out of fear, the Egyptians enslaved the Israelites. The story of Moses begins 350 years after God established His covenant with Abraham.

His story begins at his birth during a time in Egypt when the Pharaoh had ordered all the male Hebrew[5] babies be put to death. His Levite[6] mother and father spared his life and his mother kept him hidden for three months. When she could hide him no longer, she placed him in a wicker basket and set him among the reeds in the Nile. He was then discovered and saved by the Pharaoh's daughter.

In a beautiful turn of events, Moses' birth mother was selected to be his nursemaid, as Pharaoh's daughter was unable to perform the task. Moses was with his mother until he was weaned. From that day on, he was raised in the royal court of Egypt.

One may believe that to be a real blessing for Moses as he was well educated, and most may want to assume he lived a life of privilege. The historical account from Exodus doesn't give much detail; however, I believe there is enough evidence to suggest that life wasn't necessarily so simple for the young Hebrew boy being raised in the royal court of a people who enslaved his brethren.

Read Genesis 43:30-32. Joseph, a Hebrew and great-grandson of Abraham was the number two man in Egypt in these verses. What does verse 32 tell us about how the Egyptians regarded the Hebrews, regardless of their rank in Egypt?

_____

_____

_____

Identity   Though the Bible doesn't state when Moses was clued in to the fact that he was not actually Egyptian, we do know he was enlightened to this fact at some point because Exodus 2 tells us Moses went out to his people and "looked on their hard labors" (Ex. 2:11). The account goes on to tell us he went on to kill an Egyptian who was beating a Hebrew, and then he hid the Egyptian's body in the sand. We can safely deduce the Egyptian was one of many taskmasters over the Hebrews. In terms of his position, he was probably very easily replaced.

One might expect the slave-driving leader of a great nation like Egypt to scold his grandson for such a deed and maybe even punish him severely. Then again, when the ruler is a ruthless man who would have newborn babies killed, we might expect that he wouldn't make much of it other than to tell his grandson to handle it differently next time. That isn't what happened though. Instead, the Bible tells us, "When Pharaoh heard of this matter, he tried to kill Moses" (Ex. 2:15).

Perhaps the life of privilege is a bit of a myth. Perhaps a more likely scenario is the story of a young Hebrew boy with a speech impediment who was treated as the misfit that wasn't ever fully accepted in the royal court and not really taken in by his true brethren. Moreover, when his life was in danger, he fled to the wilderness of Midian where he got married and tended the sheep of his father-in-law for 40 years.

Can you imagine the identity crisis experienced by this man Moses? He was caught somewhere in the middle of who he was raised to be and who he actually was. He was cast away by his slave woman mother, who in turn got to nurse him until he was ready to be adopted by the daughter of the most powerful man in the land. He was raised to worship the gods of Egypt, but never fully learned the religious customs of his own people. Until he killed the Egyptian taskmaster, he was a "man of power in words and deeds" (Acts 7:22) and then he became prey for Pharaoh's hunt.

Modern psychiatrists would be chomping at the bit to have this man on their couches. Moses spent 40 years sorting things out in the sheep-tending solitude of the Midian wilderness. Then, Moses encounters The Creator, Who taught Moses two things. God answered the question Moses anticipates from the Israelites regarding the name of the one who sent him with the words, "I AM WHO I AM," and thus revealed His own identity to Moses. And over the course of time, Moses learned from God Almighty that whoever Moses believed himself to be mattered little when compared with the man God Almighty told Moses he was to be.

Identity plays a huge part in the Mosaic covenant. Oftentimes, we use the phrase, "how I define myself" when we talk about our identities.

Take time to write down and discuss some ways that you identify or define yourself. Also, write down and discuss some ways that you identify or define God.

_____

_____

_____

_____

Deliverer

After much discussion and reassurance from The Lord God, Moses accepted his calling to take the Word of God to Pharaoh and bring the sons of Israel out of Egypt. He reunited, and shared the Word of the Lord with his brother, Aaron. Aaron was given permission by God to speak for Moses as Moses was concerned about his speech abilities due to a speech impediment. Having returned to Egypt, he went before the people of Israel and performed the miraculous signs God had given him to perform before the people, and the people believed.

With the support of the people of Israel, Moses and Aaron went before Pharaoh and made their requests known regarding the Israelites. They asked that they be allowed to go celebrate a feast to the Lord God in the wilderness. Pharaoh, in turn, increased the labor of the Israelites. After Pharaoh's harsh response to Moses and the Israelites, God and Moses had another conversation. It was in this conversation where the Abrahamic covenant was remembered and God began to reveal, in part, the establishment of the covenant with Israel.

Exodus 6:2-8

God spoke further to Moses and said to him, "I am the LORD; ³and I appeared to Abraham, Isaac, and Jacob, as God Almighty, but by My name, LORD, I did not make Myself known to them. ⁴"I also established My covenant with them, to give them the land of Canaan, the land in which they sojourned. [5] *"Furthermore I have heard the groaning of the sons of Israel, because the Egyptians are holding them in bondage, and I have remembered My covenant.* [6] *"Say, therefore, to the sons of Israel, 'I am the* LORD, *and I will bring you out from under the burdens of the Egyptians, and I will deliver you from their bondage. I will also redeem you with an outstretched arm and with great judgments.* [7] *'Then I will take you for My people, and I will be your God; and you shall know that I am the* LORD *your God, who brought you out from under the burdens of the Egyptians.* [8] *'I will bring you to the land which I swore to give to Abraham, Isaac, and Jacob, and I will give it to you for a possession; I am the* LORD.*'"*

In these words, God revealed Himself first, and then He revealed who the sons of Israel were to become. How did God reveal Himself? (vv. 3 and 6)

_____

_____

_____

When we see the word LORD spelled in all capital letters in the Old Testament, you can be certain that this is a replacement word for "YHWH." In Jewish culture it is the most reverent name for The Lord God. It has been translated as Jehovah, and we usually pronounce this YHWH spelling, Yahweh. (Yah-Way) This passage presents a peculiar moment for us as God states, "but by My name, LORD, I did not make Myself known to them" (Ex.6:3). This is peculiar because we can see LORD in the book of Genesis: Chapter 15:7 (Jehovah), Chapter 22:14 (*Jehovah-jireh*, the LORD provides), and Genesis 28:13 (*Jehovah-Elohim*, the One True God). God was certainly known by Abraham, Isaac, and Jacob as a being of might and power, but did they really know the full extent of His being? In Exodus 3, God calls Himself, I AM WHO I AM. He then goes on to instruct Moses to tell the sons of Israel, "I AM has sent me to you" (Ex. 3:14).

What does this revelation of His name, I AM, tell us about God that wasn't known prior to His revelation to Moses?

_____

_____

_____

This is perhaps my favorite aspect of God and has been for many years. The name I AM is such a revealing name. In our worldly lives, we've all encountered the question numerous times,

"Does God exist?" In His name, the question is so simply answered as an absolute. The answer is YES, because He told us, "I AM." He is an absolute existence. His name leaves nothing to doubt. While this revelation is awesome in and of itself, His name goes so much deeper. I AM can be placed before so many of His attributes. I AM Provider, I AM Redeemer, I AM Comforter, I AM Deliverer, I AM Judge, I AM Counselor, the list goes on and on. Forever and always He is I AM, not I WAS, not I WILL BE, not I MIGHT BE, not I USED TO BE, but I AM. His own name sings His praises and glorifies Him. There was nothing before Him, and there will be nothing after Him, because He is eternal and immutable. He is because He said, "I AM," and He cannot go against His Word.

After God revealed Himself, who did He reveal the sons of Israel are to become?

_____

_____

Up to this point, God had not revealed Himself to very many people. It was just a few people at a time that had been graced with His presence. Never before had God revealed Himself to a nation. It is important to keep in mind that the sons of Israel did not identify themselves as God's people. They knew very little about God, other than the promises He made to Abraham and his descendants. Imagine the identity crises that must have been in place after all those years of slavery. Imagine the questions being posed by the people as they are beaten down, whipped, and mocked by their taskmasters. Was this God who spoke to Abraham for real? Would He really come through on His promise? That blessing, as they were enslaved in Egypt, must have seemed rather insignificant, but they remained hopeful and faithful enough to, at the very least, call upon the God of Abraham.

Why did God reveal Himself first and then reveal that the sons of Israel were to become His people afterward? Why should this order matter?

_____

_____

_____

God instructed Moses to tell the people, ". . . I will also redeem you with an outstretched arm . . ." (Ex. 6:6). The outstretched arm was an indication to the sons of Israel that God was going to take   **Redeemer** action and deliver them from the enemy who enslaved them with power and might. The word "redeem" is used in the Bible a few ways. Redeem can simply mean "to pay the ransom." In this instance in Exodus, it meant "to act as a kinsmen."

Read Galatians 3:13. What did Jesus do with two outstretched arms on the cross?

_____

_____

For the purpose of this study, a number of chapters are going to be left out, regretfully. It is highly recommended that you take time on your own to read through these chapters as the story is incomplete without them and ultimately, Bible study needs to be about exposing ourselves to God's written Word.

As the story progresses, God uses Moses and Aaron to perform miracles before Pharaoh. He uses them to call forth the plagues and, each time, Pharaoh's heart is hardened toward Israel. In chapter 12 we encounter the Passover. It is the final straw for Pharaoh and the Egyptians. The first born of man and beasts in all the land of Egypt are put to death by the Spirit of The Lord God.

It is called the Passover because the Israelites were instructed to smear the blood of a 1-year-old, unblemished lamb on their doorposts and lintel. This was a sign to the Spirit to pass over that home, and the first born in that home were saved. Even Pharaoh lost his first born. While the sons of Israel had already begun to believe in and worship the Lord God, this was their first act of obedience to His instruction. This act of obedience led to the salvation of all of Israel's first born. This act saved them from God's judgment, as His Spirit would see the blood of the lamb and recognize the people as His.

Following the Passover, Pharaoh released the sons of Israel. In chapter 13, God led the people out of Egypt as a pillar of cloud by day and as a pillar of fire by night. Pharaoh's pride and stubbornness got the best of him, and he eventually pursued the sons of Israel. His army caught up as they approached the Red Sea, and it is there, in chapter 14, that God commands Moses, ". . . lift up your staff and stretch out your hand over the sea and divide it . . ." (Ex. 14:16). The sons of Israel passed safely through on dry land. However, Pharaoh's army made the fatal error of following them and God released the waters to cover them so "not even one of them remained" (Ex. 14:28). The Bible goes on to tell us, "When Israel saw the great power which the LORD had used against the Egyptians, the people feared the LORD, and they believed in the LORD and in His servant Moses" (Ex. 14:31).

The journey through the wilderness continued for Israel with moments of grumbling and quarreling by the people. During that time, God revealed more about Himself to the people and added to His name. He became *Jehovah-rapha'* (LORD, I AM Healer) as He sweetened the waters at Marah (ch. 15), *Jehovah-jireh* (LORD, I AM Provider) as He brought forth manna and sent in the quail for food (ch. 16), and *Jehovah-nissi* (The LORD is My Banner) as Moses raised his hands in intercession while Joshua led the men to battle against Amalek (ch. 17).

The sons of Israel had been out of Egypt for three months, being led by God. God's hand was on His prophet, Moses, and through him, God revealed Himself, both as God Almighty and as a caretaker for Israel. God revealed that He made a distinction between Israel and all other peoples. It was then, as Israel reached the Sinai wilderness and set up camp at the base of the mountain, that they were ready to go into a deeper relationship with the Lord God.

Exodus 19:3-9

³*Moses went up to God, and the LORD called to him from the mountain, saying, "Thus you shall say to the house of Jacob and tell the sons of Israel:* ⁴*'You yourselves have seen what I did to the Egyptians, and how I bore you on eagles' wings, and brought you to Myself.* ⁵*'Now then, if you will indeed obey My voice and keep My covenant, then you shall be My own possession among all the peoples, for all the earth is Mine;* ⁶*and you shall be to Me a kingdom of priests and a holy nation.' These are the words that you shall speak to the sons of Israel."*

⁷*So Moses came and called the elders of the people, and set before them all these words which the LORD had commanded him.* ⁸*All the people answered together and said, "All that the LORD has spoken we will do!" And Moses brought back the words of the people to the LORD.* ⁹*The LORD said to Moses, "Behold, I will come to you in a thick cloud, so that the people may hear when I speak with you and may also believe in you forever." Then Moses told the words of the people to the LORD.*

This covenant displays a language that exhibits a cause and effect relationship. This is the first of the Biblical covenants to actually do that. You can see the relationship by use of the words "if" and "then." This is known as a conditional covenant. The people have to meet certain conditions in order for the covenant to be fulfilled.

What condition must the Israelites meet? (This is the "if" in the covenant.) What is their reward? (This is the "then" in the covenant.)

If . . .

Then . . .

The Mosaic Covenant

Did God promise the people any sort of material goods?

_____

. . . Is

Yours

After being enslaved in Egypt and subsequently being freed from being Pharaoh's possession, why do you suppose the Israelites were willing to enter this covenant and become a "possession" once again?

_____

_____

_____

Read Matthew 6:19; James 5:3. How does God view your earthly possessions?

_____

_____

_____

For three months, the people had been in the desert where there were no crops to sustain them. They had no land there. They had enemies attack them. They were thirsty and encountered undrinkable water. Yet, in all these things, God sustained them. They had no other explanation. There was no way they could possibly claim credit for their miraculous success. They saw God's power and were fully immersed in His sustenance. Because of Him, they could survive and thrive in uninhabitable places. God had spent three months revealing Himself to them, showing them that being His and being with Him is worth vastly more than any material things.

In our culture, we tend to celebrate self-reliance. What did God desire from Israel?

_____

What got established in three months with Israel that allowed them to submit to being God's possession? Have you allowed God to establish that in your life? What has to be in place for Him to establish this in your life?

_____

_____

_____

When Moses finally submitted to God, what did he ultimately receive, which he had been confused about? When Israel submitted to God, what did they ultimately receive? What do we receive when we fully submit to Him? Read Luke 3:21-22 What did Jesus receive from God when He publicly submitted? (Hint: they all have the same answer.)

The revelation of God's nature, power and character was ingrained and established with Israel. Just as Israel spent time with Him, we too must spend time with God, His Word, for Him to reveal Who He fully is. This is a conscious choice we make. God does not force His way into your life, but He does continually call to you. When we submit to Him, He claims us for His own, and we receive a spirit of adoption and an irrefutable identity. That is so much more than any singular thing we can receive. He tells Moses, "The earth is Mine" (Ex. 19:5).

After all this time of God revealing Himself, the Bible tells us, ". . . Moses brought the people out of the camp to meet God . . ." (Ex. 19:17). This was after Israel accepted the covenant. Israel accepted the terms of a covenant with a being they had never met. They had seen the works of His hand. They had seen His power at work. They followed His servant and His pillar of cloud/fire. But one thing remained undone prior to their acceptance. They had never met God. All the Words spoken by God were for Moses and directed only to his ears. This conditional covenant was accepted solely on faith.

As God stated in the covenant agreement, there were commands. Therefore, the next step in the unfolding of the covenant was the revelation of the commands, which governed three aspects of their lives: 1.) The Ten Commandments are presented first in Exodus 20:1-26. The Ten Commandments governed their personal lives as they related to God. At the very least, take time to read through chapter 20. 2.) In Exodus 21:1–24:11 God gave commands which governed the social lives of the Israelites as they related to one another. They address such matters as personal injuries, property rights, various sundry laws, a sabbatical year for land, and national feasts. 3.) In Exodus 24:12–31:18 and much of the book of Leviticus, God provided commands which governed their religious lives so they knew how to approach God on His terms.[7]

The Old Covenant

The commands of the covenant are known as The Law. Later on, when we study the New Covenant, you may ask yourself, "What is the Old Covenant?" The Mosaic covenant, which includes the Law, is the Old Covenant. Throughout the Old Testament, God refers back to His covenant that He made with Israel. This covenant is central to the story of the Old Testament. This covenant was known throughout the nations of Israel. It was this covenant to which the prophets called the people to repent and return.

The Mosaic Covenant

Let's quickly paraphrase the Ten Commandments:

- Have no other gods before Me.

- Don't make idols/graven images

- Don't take the name of the LORD your God in vain.

- Remember the Sabbath and keep it holy.

- Honor your father and mother.

- Don't murder.

- Don't commit adultery.

- Don't steal.

- Don't bear false witness against your neighbor.

- Don't covet your neighbor's stuff.

Around whom do the first four commandments revolve? In other words, who comes first?

Around whom do the last six commandments revolve?

What does this order tell you about your primary concerns and secondary concerns?

_____

_____

_____

How does the tenth commandment relate to the reward part of the covenant, being God's possession?

_____

_____

_____

The Ten Commandments are, for all intents and purposes, the top ten list. That the last six listings are even in the top ten should make these primary concerns. That said, if you take the first four seriously and are faithful to God's commands regarding Himself, you are far more likely to regard His last six commands as holy ordinance as well. We can easily look around us in our world and in our culture and see that as a society we still tend to frown on murder, theft and lying. What about the other 7 commands, how are they doing in our world view?

How many times have you heard someone say, "I know I shouldn't covet, but . . ." or "I know I shouldn't be jealous, but . . ."? I don't want to implicate all people in my sin, but most of us have said it ourselves or, at the very least, thought it. We tend to give coveting a free pass. Material rewards are not what this covenant was about. It was about being His and being with Him. When we focus on the material rewards, the material becomes our graven image. When we say, "I know I'm not supposed to, but . . ." we are taking His commandments, His Word, in vain.

While we are looking at coveting, let's look at one other aspect of it that often gets passed over in Old Testament studies. So often in studying the Old Testament, we focus on the external conduct of the characters. Coveting, unlike the rest of the Ten Commandments, is an internal condition. It is an issue of character, the root from which external behaviors spring forth.

Take a look at the following verse and write down what Paul asks the Philippians to focus on in order to be Christ-like.

Philippians 2:5

_____

_____

_____

What are your internal struggles that lead to sinful behaviors/choices in your life?

_____

_____

_____

The second area of governance in the law covered ordinances specifically for the purpose of governing the social lives of the Israelites and how they related to one another. God covered a lot of possible issues that may have come up between the people regarding behavior. If a law is in place, establishing standard consequences and administering justice, what will this help to prevent between two parties that are at odds?

_____

_____

_____

Covenant Reveals HIM and HIS People

The Mosaic Covenant

With these ordinances in place, God was able to head off potential chaos and bring order to the people. What did this do for outsiders looking in on the nation of Israel and their perception of the Israelites? (See Ex. 19:6.)

_____

_____

_____

In the final area of governance, God provided commands which governed how they were to approach Him. Read Exodus 30:20-21; Exodus 30:8-9; Leviticus 10:1-2. What purpose did this third area of governance serve for the Israelites in approaching their holy God?

_____

_____

_____

Earlier in the chapter, we learned how God revealed Himself as _Jehovah-jireh_ (LORD Provider), _Jehovah-nissi_ (The LORD is my Banner), and _Jehovah-rapha_ (LORD Healer). With Abraham, God revealed Himself as a "shield" and as _El-Shaddai_ (God Almighty). How do you see these names being revealed in the three areas of governance?

_____

_____

_____

For a fully detailed description of the tabernacle, you can read Exodus 24:12–31:18. Another, shorter description exists in Hebrews 9:1-10. (We'll visit this Scripture in the final chapter.) To sum up the tabernacle and its ordinances, let me offer these brief words. The tabernacle had two significant areas of holiness. The area encompassed by the outer veil was known as the Holy Place and the area encompassed by the inner veil was known as the Holy of Holies. Only the priests were allowed into the Holy Place, and it was there that the priests would continually lift up divine worship. Only the high priest was allowed to enter the Holy of Holies, and he was allowed only once per year to offer blood offerings for the atonement of sins.

As we saw earlier in Exodus 30:20-21, Aaron and his sons were required to wash and cleanse themselves before entering the Holy Place. Failure to do so resulted in death. In Jesus' death, the veil of the tabernacle was torn, and we are now allowed to enter into the holy presence of God.

Read 1 John 1:7,9. How has Jesus prepared us to be in the holy presence of God?

_____

_____

_____

Leviticus 26:3-13   Obedience

³'If you walk in My statutes and keep My commandments so as to carry them out, ⁴then I shall give you rains in their season, so that the land will yield its produce and the trees of the field will bear their fruit. ⁵'Indeed, your threshing will last for you until grape gathering, and grape gathering will last until sowing time. You will thus eat your food to the full and live securely in your land. ⁶'I shall also grant peace in the land, so that you may lie down with no one making you tremble. I shall also eliminate harmful beasts from the land, and no sword will pass through your land. ⁷'But you will chase your enemies and they will fall before you by the sword; ⁸five of you will chase a hundred, and a hundred of you will chase ten thousand, and your enemies will fall before you by the sword. ⁹'So I will turn toward you and make you fruitful and multiply you, and I will confirm My covenant with you. ¹⁰'You will eat the old supply and clear out the old because of the new. ¹¹'Moreover, I will make My dwelling among you, and My soul will not reject you. ¹²'I will also walk among you and be your God, and you shall be My people. ¹³'I am the LORD your God, who brought you out of the land of Egypt so that you would not be their slaves, and I broke the bars of your yoke and made you walk erect.

After giving numerous laws and ordinances, God speaks His final words regarding obedience and disobedience within the covenant in Leviticus 26. As you look specifically at vv. 3-5, what are the material rewards for obedience?

_____

_____

_____

As you look at vv. 6-12, what are the relational rewards for their obedience?

_____

_____

_____

_____

The Mosaic Covenant

What reminder does God give Israel in v. 13?

_____

_____

Isn't it interesting how God reminds them, once again, of His name and Who He is? When you are struggling with God's calling in your life and looking around wondering how things are actually going to work out, there is no greater contentment you can find than to truly know that He is God. It is during those times when you turn to His Word and read about who He is: Provider, Healer, your Banner, your Shield, and God Almighty.

Read Ezekiel 36:27; Romans 8:9; Romans 8:11; Romans 8:15; Galatians 5:22. What are some of the benefits (relational rewards) of God's dwelling in you?

_____

_____

_____

_____

_____

Disobedience   In Leviticus 26:14-39, we are shown that just as there are great rewards for obedience, there are grave consequences for disobedience. Many of the consequences are difficult to stomach as you read them. Wherein there were numerous blessings for obedience, disobedience brings numerous curses directly opposing each blessing.

Leviticus 26:40-45

⁴⁰_'If they confess their iniquity and the iniquity of their forefathers, in their unfaithfulness which they committed against Me, and also in their acting with hostility against Me—_ ⁴¹_I also was acting with hostility against them, to bring them into the land of their enemies—or if their uncircumcised heart becomes humbled so that they then make amends for their iniquity,_ ⁴²_then I will remember My covenant with Jacob, and I will remember also My covenant with Isaac, and My covenant with Abraham as well, and I will remember the land._ ⁴³_'For the land will be abandoned by them, and will make up for its sabbaths while it is made desolate without them. They, meanwhile, will be making amends for their iniquity, because they rejected My ordinances and their soul abhorred My statutes._ ⁴⁴_'Yet in spite of this, when they are in the land of their enemies, I will not reject them, nor will I so abhor them as to destroy them, breaking My covenant with them; for I am the LORD their God._ ⁴⁵_'But I will remember for them the_

covenant with their ancestors, whom I brought out of the land of Egypt in the sight of the nations, that I might be their God. I am the LORD.'"

If, in their disobedience, they confessed their iniquity or made amends for their iniquity, what did God promise to do? (See v. 42.)

_____

_____

_____

Many centuries later, the nation Israel found herself in Babylon, being held captive and making amends for her many indiscretions/iniquities. Read Jeremiah 29:10-14. What words did God have for His people, and how do they relate back to Leviticus 26? What does this tell you about God's Word?

_____

_____

_____

HE is Faithful

Even in their captivity, God was seeing to the welfare of His people and remembering His covenant with Jacob, Isaac, and Abraham and the land. During their captivity the land lay fallow for 70 years in observance of all the missed sabbatical years. It really makes sense when you think about it. How could the land be fallow for 70 years if the people were living in the land? They would have no food during that time. Granted, God could resort back to manna, but He promised in Leviticus that they would be handed over to their enemies for their disobedience.

The Mosaic covenant, while considered a conditional covenant, has one aspect that is unconditional. The nation of Israel experienced blessings and curses depending on their actions and how they did or did not revere God. Through all the blessings and curses though, one thing remained without condition. God never stopped being the God of Israel. The nation may have been in a season of rebellion with their backs turned toward Him, but when they were ready to repent and return to their identity as God's people, He was always there, always ready to receive them.

What does this reveal to you about who God is and where He is when you are caught up in sin?

_____

_____

_____

Closing Reflections

What struggles do you encounter that stand in the way of letting God reveal more and more about Himself to you?

What role is your self-identity playing in the area of allowing God to define you and revealing His purpose for you?

We might call Him Lord or Father, and perhaps a few other names, but we have a tendency to think of God in terms of the name "God." Write out a prayer, or at least pray a prayer, using the various names God revealed to Israel and Abraham: Provider, Healer, Banner, your Shield, and God Almighty. (You can use the Hebrew names. They won't make the prayer any more holy, but there is a certain degree of intimacy that comes with them.)

Join the Conversation on:

Facebook: facebook.com/Thecovenantschristandyou Like and Post your thoughts on God's covenant with Moses and the people of Israel.

  or

Twitter: @CovChristU Tweet your thoughts on God's covenant with Moses and the people of Israel.

Engaging Others:

Tweet it, Post it, Pin it, or Instagram a picture of something that represents your God-given identity. If that is different from who you perceive yourself to be, pair it with another picture of that object/thing. Then write a short reflection. Tweet it to @CovChristU or Tag the Facebook page.

Continue praying for those in your sphere of influence. Pray for God to continue calling them until they turn into His presence, much like Moses did when he finally heard God calling from the burning bush.

Chapter 6
The Davidic Covenant

Are you the one who should build Me a house to dwell in?

—2 Samuel 7:5

God had a plan for Israel, and He allowed them to enter into a covenant with Him. For 400 years He reigned as the King of Israel. For those 400 years, there was no human that served as King. What God did put in place over those 400 years were the judges. The time of the judges is bookended by two men who served not only as judges, but as prophets. Moses served as the first judge and Samuel served as the final judge; however, they are not included in the book of Judges, which tells of 12 judges God raised up to guide His people. Of the 12 judges, you are most likely familiar with Gideon and Samson, but the others don't seem to garner nearly as much attention in current church circles.

The judges were not a constant. That is, the death of one judge didn't lead directly into the reign of the next judge. There was a period of time after each of the judges where God tested Israel and allowed them to practice obedience or fall into disobedience.

Judges 2:16-19

Then the LORD raised up judges who delivered them from the hands of those who plundered them. ¹⁷Yet they did not listen to their judges, for they played the harlot after other gods and bowed themselves down to them. They turned aside quickly from the way in which their fathers had walked in obeying the commandments of the LORD; they did not do as their fathers. ¹⁸When the LORD raised up judges for them, the LORD was with the judge and delivered them from the hand of their enemies all the days of the judge; for the LORD was moved to pity by their groaning because of those who oppressed and afflicted them. [19]But it came about when the judge died, that they would turn back and act more corruptly than their fathers, in following other gods to serve them and bow down to them; they did not abandon their practices or their stubborn ways.

There is no mention of Joshua, who followed after Moses, or of Eli, who preceded Samuel, being judges themselves. Whether they were or not is of little consequence for this study, but what does matter is the simple fact that the only King of Israel for those 400 years was God.

Sadly, the judge and prophet Samuel received word from the elders of Israel, rejecting God as their King and demanding an earthly king like all the other nations surrounding them. This was an extremely critical moment in the history of Israel and it is a moment that must be understood to fully appreciate the purpose of God's covenant with David.

Give Us a King to Judge

This critical moment occurs in 1 Samuel 8. First, let's take a look at how this moment unfolded. Then we'll take a look at how this moment was supposed to unfold. For, you see, God planned for this time and He revealed His plan to Moses, in Deuteronomy 17.

1 Samuel 8:4-20

[4]Then all the elders of Israel gathered together and came to Samuel at Ramah; [5]and they said to him, "Behold, you have grown old, and your sons do not walk in your ways. Now appoint a king for us to judge us like all the nations." [6]But the thing was displeasing in the sight of Samuel when they said, "Give us a king to judge us." And Samuel prayed to the LORD. [7]The LORD said to Samuel, "Listen to the voice of the people in regard to all that they say to you, for they have not rejected you, but they have rejected Me from being king over them. [8]"Like all the deeds which they have done since the day that I brought them up from Egypt even to this day—in that they have forsaken Me and served other gods—so they are doing to you also. [9]"Now then, listen to their voice; however, you shall solemnly warn them and tell them of the procedure of the king who will reign over them." [10]So Samuel spoke all the words of the LORD to the people who had asked of him a king. [11]He said, "This will be the procedure of the king who will reign over you: he will take your sons and place them for himself in his chariots and among his horsemen and they will run before his chariots. [12]"He will appoint for himself commanders of thousands and of fifties, and some to do his plowing and to reap his harvest and to make his weapons of war and equipment for his chariots. [13]"He will also take your daughters for perfumers and cooks and bakers. [14]"He will take the best of your fields and your vineyards and your olive groves and give them to his servants. [15]"He will take a tenth of your seed and of your vineyards and give to his officers and to his servants. [16]"He will also take your male servants and your female servants and your best young men and your donkeys and use them for his work. [17]"He will take a

tenth of your flocks, and you yourselves will become his servants. ¹⁸*"Then you will cry out in that day because of your king whom you have chosen for yourselves, but the* LORD *will not answer you in that day."* ¹⁹*Nevertheless, the people refused to listen to the voice of Samuel, and they said, "No, but there shall be a king over us,* ²⁰*that we also may be like all the nations, that our king may judge us and go out before us and fight our battles."*

Deuteronomy 17:14-20

¹⁴*"When you enter the land which the* LORD *your God gives you, and you possess it and live in it, and you say, 'I will set a king over me like all the nations who are around me,'* ¹⁵*you shall surely set a king over you whom the* LORD *your God chooses, one from among your countrymen you shall set as king over yourselves; you may not put a foreigner over yourselves who is not your countryman.* ¹⁶*"Moreover, he shall not multiply horses for himself, nor shall he cause the people to return to Egypt to multiply horses, since the* LORD *has said to you, 'You shall never again return that way.'* ¹⁷*"He shall not multiply wives for himself, or else his heart will turn away; nor shall he greatly increase silver and gold for himself.* ¹⁸*"Now it shall come about when he sits on the throne of his kingdom, he shall write for himself a copy of this law on a scroll in the presence of the Levitical priests.* ¹⁹*"It shall be with him and he shall read it all the days of his life, that he may learn to fear the* LORD *his God, by carefully observing all the words of this law and these statutes,* ²⁰*that his heart may not be lifted up above his countrymen and that he may not turn aside from the commandment, to the right or the left, so that he and his sons may continue long in his kingdom in the midst of Israel.*

Take a close look at Deuteronomy 17:14 and 1 Samuel 8:5-6. How does the request of the elders in Samuel differ from what God said they should request in Deuteronomy?

_____

_____

_____

God clearly states to Samuel that Israel had rejected God, not Samuel. By asking for a "king to judge," what else are they rejecting, other than just God Himself? Why is the request for a judge such a big deal? It is, after all, just one extra word.

_____

_____

_____

The Davidic Covenant

Read 1 Samuel 8:11-17. List the attributes of the king Samuel describes to Israel.

_____

_____

_____

_____

_____

_____

_____

_____

Read Deuteronomy 17:15-20. List the attributes of the king God describes.

_____

_____

_____

_____

_____

_____

_____

_____

_____

The elders of Israel accepted the terms Samuel presented to them. What does this tell you about their knowledge and devotion to God's Word? Knowing God's Word, what would be the obvious response to such terms as Samuel presented?

_____

_____

We've listed the attributes of the king Samuel describes in 2 Samuel. As you consider this list and reflect on Israel's past, of whom or what does this kingly description remind you?

_____

_____

We've listed the attributes of the king God describes in Deuteronomy. Take another look at that list. Consider this description as a word painting of the king. Describe this king in your own words.

_____

_____

Had the elders been mindful of what sort of king God wished to place before them, they never would have accepted the terms Samuel presented. They fell victim to their lack of devotion to God, His Word, and His Law. Quite simply, they rejected not only God, they rejected His Law, in essence saying, "Your Law isn't good enough for us." They really wanted to be like everyone else around them, not the holy people God called His own.

The king Samuel presented is, very much, an enslaving king. Israel essentially asked for, and accepted, a return to their former enslavement in Egypt. They may not have asked to physically return to Egypt, but the circumstances were very close to the same. God's intention was a humble servant, unlike any other king. The king God desired was going to be devoted to the Law of the Lord God. He would be devoted to the Word of God. God's intention, all along, was Jesus.

Despite the king described by Samuel, God set in place a man named Saul to serve as the first king of Israel. Saul had all the potential in the world to be a king who more closely resembled the king God described in Deuteronomy instead of the king Samuel described. Despite the potential, Saul violated the Lord's command in two acts of disobedience. In his rebuking that proceeded from Saul's disobedient sacrifice, Samuel tells him, ". . . you have not kept the commandment of the Lord your God, which He commanded you, for now the Lord would have established your kingdom over Israel forever" (1 Sam. 13:13). Sadly for Saul, not only was he disobedient with the sacrifice in chapter 13, he fell into further disobedience two chapters later when he failed to carry out the express command of the Lord, from the mouth of Samuel, as he led his army against the Amalekites. After his second act of disobedience, Samuel states, ". . . The Lord has torn the kingdom of Israel from you today . . ." (1 Sam. 15:28). Saul failed to be devoted to the Word of God. Although David was the next king and God established His covenant with David, keep in mind that every king that reigned over Israel following Saul, including the ones

Woulda, Coulda, Shoulda

that were considered righteous by God, managed to have at least one flaw that kept them from being the king God described in Deuteronomy.

As each of the kings of Israel would have a flaw that would leave them short of being the king God wanted to put in place, a covenant was necessary to let His people know that He is faithful to His Word. God wanted to establish this covenant with Saul, but Saul showed a lack of obedience to God's Word, exhibiting a willingness to hear the Word, but not to follow it. Samuel told Saul, ". . . for now the LORD *would have* established your kingdom over Israel forever. But now your kingdom shall not endure. The LORD has sought out for Himself a man after His own heart, and the LORD has appointed him as ruler over His people" (1 Sam. 13:13-14). God found in David "a man after His own heart" and established His covenant with David.

Everlasting Kingdom   This covenant is shown four times in Scripture. Twice the covenant is stated by God, through the prophet Nathan. The other two accounts are retellings by David, once to Solomon and the other to the officials of Israel. We will focus on two of these accounts in this study, but I would encourage you to read all four accounts. The covenant presentations are found in 2 Samuel 7:1-16; 1 Chronicles 17:1-15; 1 Chronicles 22:6-13; and 1 Chronicle 28:1-7.

David served as king for 40 years. The first 7 years of his kingship, David was the king of Judah. After that, Israel and Judah were re-united, and David served as king over all of Israel for 33 years. It was soon after the re-uniting that David determined to bring the Ark of the Covenant to Jerusalem. The ark had been in Baale-judah, literally, the center of Baal worship in Judah. The story of moving the ark is found in 2 Samuel 6. It was in the very next chapter that God established His covenant with David.

As a frame of reference it should be noted that the establishment of the covenant was done at a time when David had three sons. It also preceded David's most infamous treacheries: his sin with Bathsheba, murdering Uriah, and his census. These heinous acts may seem to be good reasons for God to choose someone else or declare the covenant null and void to our minds, but He doesn't do those things. God's thoughts are not our thoughts, and His ways are not our ways. Many people want to burn with anger toward David for his despicable actions, and this can be a true stumbling block in our Christian walk as we want so badly to impose our own personal will upon our Holy God. As you read God's Word, allow the Holy Spirit to reveal who God is as you study. Find contentment in the fact that God is not bound by our decisions and His ultimate purpose will be accomplished.

2 Samuel 7:1-16

Now it came about when the king lived in his house, and the LORD had given him rest on every side from all his enemies, ²that the king said to Nathan the prophet, "See now,

I dwell in a house of cedar, but the ark of God dwells within tent curtains." ³Nathan said to the king, "Go, do all that is in your mind, for the LORD is with you."

⁴But in the same night the word of the LORD came to Nathan, saying, ⁵"Go and say to My servant David, 'Thus says the LORD, "Are you the one who should build Me a house to dwell in? ⁶"For I have not dwelt in a house since the day I brought up the sons of Israel from Egypt, even to this day; but I have been moving about in a tent, even in a tabernacle. ⁷"Wherever I have gone with all the sons of Israel, did I speak a word with one of the tribes of Israel, which I commanded to shepherd My people Israel, saying, 'Why have you not built Me a house of cedar?'"

⁸"Now therefore, thus you shall say to My servant David, 'Thus says the LORD of hosts, "I took you from the pasture, from following the sheep, to be ruler over My people Israel. ⁹"I have been with you wherever you have gone and have cut off all your enemies from before you; and I will make you a great name, like the names of the great men who are on the earth. ¹⁰"I will also appoint a place for My people Israel and will plant them, that they may live in their own place and not be disturbed again, nor will the wicked afflict them any more as formerly, ¹¹even from the day that I commanded judges to be over My people Israel; and I will give you rest from all your enemies. The LORD also declares to you that the LORD will make a house for you. ¹²"When your days are complete and you lie down with your fathers, I will raise up your descendant after you, who will come forth from you, and I will establish his kingdom. ¹³"He shall build a house for My name, and I will establish the throne of his kingdom forever. ¹⁴"I will be a father to him and he will be a son to Me; when he commits iniquity, I will correct him with the rod of men and the strokes of the sons of men, ¹⁵but My lovingkindness shall not depart from him, as I took it away from Saul, whom I removed from before you. ¹⁶"Your house and your kingdom shall endure before Me forever; your throne shall be established forever."'

As we can see, David recognized the discrepancy in his house of cedar and the tent where God's presence resided on the ark. What does David's intention to build a permanent dwelling for God reveal to you about David? According to what Samuel told Saul, with what kind of man was God seeking to establish His covenant? (See 1 Samuel 13:14.)

**Man after
GOD's
Own
Heart**

_____

_____

Did God ask or command David to build Him a house?

Read James 4:13-16. What is the folly behind David's plan?

_____

_____

_____

The Davidic Covenant

I've always been amused by the saying, "Man makes plans, and God laughs." David did, in this situation, what so many Christians do out of zeal for The Lord. The issue is not that David thought up a good or bad idea, but that he did not seek God's approval.

Do you ever make plans to work for the Lord without seeking His approval and His will? What did you experience during the planning or actual labor by going forth in the process?

_____

_____

_____

Everything I Am . . .   Read Job 38:1-18. God's response to David's plans seems to have a similar tone to His response to Job. As part of His response to David, God questions, "Are you the one who should build Me a house to dwell in?' (2 Sam. 7:5) David had a fundamental misunderstanding of God's true nature.

Write down what the following Scriptures reveal about God's relationship to the house of worship.

Exodus 33:18-23

_____

_____

_____

Psalms 90:1

_____

_____

_____

Revelation 21:22-23

_____

_____

_____

The tent in which God was dwelling and the walls of the temple that Solomon would one day build were nothing but a screen to protect Israel from God's overwhelming glory. You can't build a temple to God. . . He is the Temple. You can't build a house for God . . . He is the House. You can't build anything to glorify God . . . He is the Glory.

The book of 1 Chronicles presents the covenant three times. The second time, it is presented by David as he revealed the covenant to his son, Solomon.

1 Chronicles 22:6-13

Then he called for his son Solomon, and charged him to build a house for the LORD God of Israel. ⁷David said to Solomon, "My son, I had intended to build a house to the name of the LORD my God. ⁸"But the word of the LORD came to me, saying, 'You have shed much blood and have waged great wars; you shall not build a house to My name, because you have shed so much blood on the earth before Me. ⁹'Behold, a son will be born to you, who shall be a man of rest; and I will give him rest from all his enemies on every side; for his name shall be Solomon, and I will give peace and quiet to Israel in his days. ¹⁰'He shall build a house for My name, and he shall be My son and I will be his father; and I will establish the throne of his kingdom over Israel forever.' ¹¹"Now, my son, the LORD be with you that you may be successful, and build the house of the LORD your God just as He has spoken concerning you. ¹²"Only the LORD give you discretion and understanding, and give you charge over Israel, so that you may keep the law of the LORD your God. ¹³"Then you will prosper, if you are careful to observe the statutes and the ordinances which the LORD commanded Moses concerning Israel. Be strong and courageous, do not fear nor be dismayed.

Take a look at the two excerpts showing the covenant presentations (2 Samuel and 1 Chronicles). List all the promises of the covenant. (Though it isn't necessary, you may want to highlight promises that are in one presentation, but not the other.)

. . . Is Yours

_____

_____

_____

_____

_____

_____

_____

_____

_____

_____

_____

_____

The Davidic Covenant

As mentioned earlier, this covenant was established prior to David's great treacheries. As you look at this list you just created, do you see any further requirements/responsibilities for David?

_____

_____

From the time the Ark of the Covenant was created until Solomon built the temple, God's dwelling place was in a tent. If you can think back to His covenant with Abraham, remember that God showed Abraham the land which his descendants would possess. In building a permanent house for the Lord, which part of the Abrahamic covenant was being fulfilled? (See Gen. 17:8.)

_____

_____

_____

The building of a permanent temple was a sign to all of Israel saying, this is your home. Up until the temple was built, though Jerusalem was a center for Israel, Hebron was the center for Judah. This brought, at least temporarily, a unity to the divided kingdom. Had all ordinances been met, it would have remained united. At the building of the temple, all of the house of Israel had one permanent religious center. With the exception of a time with the disobedient king, Jeroboam, the temple in Jerusalem remained the religious center for all the Israelites who did not stray away to follow other gods.

In addition to His covenant with David being fulfilled in the building of a temple, God fulfills His promise to Abraham, as this made the land a permanent dwelling place. It was a sign, not only to Israel, but to all the nations.

It should be understood that these covenants do not make previous covenants void. Instead, these covenants fulfill and expand previous covenants.

A Man of Peace Is Given   Read 2 Samuel 12:24-25. David was already a father to several sons at the time of the covenant. The initial words God spoke through the prophet, Nathan, do not mention the name Solomon. How did he determine Solomon was to be the heir to his throne?

_____

_____

_____

God called Solomon "Jedidiah," or "beloved of the LORD." This renaming of Solomon is much like a father naming a son. As we can see from the covenant, God planned to be a father to David's descendant and his descendant would be a son to God.

Further examination of the covenant promise tells us that Solomon would be a man of peace, as David was a man of war. Though we have not done so here, reading the overall story of David and his children also reveals his other sons to be men of war.

Read 2 Chronicles 7:12-22. God approached Solomon twice in order to reaffirm the covenant He made with David. This passage is from the second occurrence. Re-read verse 19 and go back and re-read God's list of attributes of the king He wished to place in Israel from Deuteronomy 17:14-20. Which guideline from Deuteronomy was critical for Solomon to fulfill his part in the covenant as you compare Deuteronomy with v. 19?

_____

_____

_____

The Law is certainly not lacking in complication and for that reason God put judges in place. However, Solomon was supernaturally gifted in the area of wisdom. He was the wisest man on earth. The Law would have been a simple matter for his understanding. Sadly for Solomon, his wisdom may have been his one stumbling block as he did not adhere to the Law/Word of God, and instead, leaned on his own understanding. If only Solomon would have known and adhered to the passage in Deuteronomy 17, he could have recognized his own role as the godly king.

While Deuteronomy 17 is fresh in your mind, read the following passages regarding Solomon's wealth: 1 Kings 3:10-13; 1 Kings 10:14-29. You may be tempted at first to condemn Solomon's accumulation of wealth, as doing so would indicate his stepping out of the bounds of Deuteronomy 17. However, to do so would be incorrect. In 1 Kings 3:13, God explained that He was giving Solomon riches and honor, though Solomon did not ask for them. Additionally, 1 Kings 10:14 and 25 both indicate the riches were brought in as a gift to Solomon. He did not take them as a tax. They were gifted to him. In other words, he did not go about increasing gold and silver for himself. In fact, he apparently spread the wealth, as verse 27 states that he made "silver as common as stones in Jerusalem. . . ." So, where did Solomon fail? Those familiar with Solomon should have no problem with the answer to that question. In case you're not familiar with the story, read 1 Kings 11:1-8.

The Davidic Covenant

What actions did Solomon take that set him clearly on a divergent path from the king God described in Deuteronomy? What was the result?

_____

_____

Because Solomon failed to adhere to God's statutes and ordinances, Israel fell into rebellion. Most of the kingdom was stripped away from the house of David, leaving only a small remnant called Judah to be led by David's descendants. Many of the kings who served in either kingdom were total failures who sought their own glory, and a few, though they had their folly, were called righteous by God. With the righteous would come blessings, peace, and rest for the nation, and with the wicked would come curses, war, and unrest for the nation. Many started out well enough, but eventually pride and arrogance would rule the day.

Nevertheless, God made a covenant with David that included one very important and lasting statement. God told David, ". . . your throne shall be established forever" (2 Sam. 7:16).

Read Luke 1:31-33. How did God plan to fulfill His covenant promise to David?

_____

_____

_____

Such a King as This

In addition to establishing David's throne forever, I find it interesting that God told David He would make his name great. He gave the same promise to Abraham. Abraham was called the father of many nations. More importantly God identifies Himself as the "God of Abraham." David is revered as a great psalmist, a great warrior, and a man after God's heart. However, that's not the greatest part of his name. David's name became known as an identifier of the Messiah. Jesus is known as the "Son of David."

Read the following verses and explain how God fulfills this covenant with David in your own life. What happens when Jesus sits upon the throne of your heart?

Colossians 3:15

_____

_____

John 14:27

_____

_____

Philippians 4:7

_____

_____

In Jesus, God has placed a King over His people who meets all the attributes God desires of the man to rule over His people. As I was writing this lesson, I began to struggle with the riches and wealth that accompanied so many of God's blessings, not only in the lives of David and Solomon, but so many of the righteous men of the Old Testament. In contemporary society, we tend to equate God's blessing with riches and material possession. Those with much in the church are often considered to be living within God's will by other believers. In fact, with many, it has become the litmus test to prove righteousness.

Jesus never put much stock in wealth. In fact, he told people to sell their possessions and give the money to the poor. Jesus had no place to lay His head. He didn't live in a palace. He didn't collect money for His miracles. David, Solomon, and many others died in their lavish palaces, or perhaps somewhat gloriously in battle. They spent their lives living as kings, just like the kings of other nations around them. Jesus spent His life as a servant and died a death reserved for the worst of criminals. Yet, His is the kingdom that will endure forever. Why?

Neither gold nor silver can compare to the majesty of God. It is in servitude, humility, and sacrifice that His Glory is revealed. Who really wants to serve a king of material wealth, as he keeps it for himself? The people grow to disdain such a man. Instead, we so greatly want to serve a king who shares His inheritance, a King whose glory fills us. Such a king, we won't want to fail. God had this King in mind all the time. Glory and honor to the One Who knows, and supplies, what we need over what we want.

Closing Reflections

What does God's plan for Israel's king, from Deuteronomy, reveal about His intentions for His people?

The Davidic Covenant

What sort of king sits upon the throne of your heart? Does that king more often resemble the king God intended or the king Samuel presented? Which king are you willing to accept?

Join the Conversation on:

Facebook: facebook.com/Thecovenantschristandyou Like and Post your thoughts on God's Covenant with David

   or

Twitter: @CovChristU Tweet your thoughts on God's covenant with David.

Engaging Others:

God can dwell in a tent or a temple made of gold and cedar. Regardless of the material, His glory fills that place. Tweet it, Post it, Pin it, or Instagram a picture of the most messy and ugly place you can find and proclaim God's ability to reach even those places. Tweet it to @CovChristU or Tag the Facebook page.

Suggested Hashtags
#Discipleship #ChristFollower #BibleStudy #SmallGroup #Evangelism #Relevant #Jesus

Keep praying for others. If you have a clear idea of the one or two people with whom you would like to share *The Covenants, Christ, and You* invite them to study it with you.

Chapter 7

The New Covenant

For I will forgive their iniquity, and their sin I will remember no more.

—Jeremiah 31:34

So very often, we listen to the communion meditation and hear the "words of institution" recited just before the communion prayer. You know the words, ". . . the Lord Jesus in the night in which He was betrayed took bread; and when He had given thanks, He broke it and said, 'This is My body, which is for you; do this in remembrance of Me.' In the same way *He took* the cup also after supper, saying, 'This cup is the new covenant in My blood; do this, as often as you drink *it,* in remembrance of Me'" (1 Cor. 11:23-25) .

We have heard these words so many times, it is easy to assume that we really know what this whole communion service is all about. It seems so very simple, doesn't it? He said, ". . . do this . . . in remembrance of Me." So that is what we do, we remember Jesus. We break and eat the bread. We drink from the cup. And we remember Jesus . . . but did we actually hear everything He was telling us?

For the longest time, I heard the words, "new covenant," and I simply understood it as Christ dying for our forgiveness, and the act of partaking in the communion was a way of showing that we've accepted forgiveness and now we're in covenant with Him. While this is definitely a glimpse into the meaning behind the observance of the Lord's supper, it falls quite short of the full meaning in the words, "new covenant"—two words, which would change everything.

As mentioned in the introduction, "covenant" is a word that makes a lot of sense in some cultures, but has a vague meaning in other cultures. Another word we use with vague meaning in the church is "kingdom." Let's, once again, simplify these words by reducing them to a couple of basic concepts.

- Covenant establishes relationship, so, covenant = relationship.
- As a believer in Christ, and one who is submitted to His will through a covenant commitment, you have kingdom responsibilities. So, kingdom = responsibility.

To further clarify, when we hear the term "covenant" in the twenty-first century, our minds revert back to an understanding of contract. Contracts are not covenants and covenants are not merely contracts. Contracts are an impersonal exchange of goods and services. Covenants, on the other hand, are about the establishment of lasting, enduring relationships, which extend beyond death (like a will). If you will recall from the introduction chapter, when two parties enter into covenant, they essentially state, "Everything I have, and everything that I am, is yours." Though the disciples didn't fully realize all that the new covenant would entail, they knew they were entering into a new type of relationship with God as they drank from the cup. They also knew that doing so would carry with it new responsibilities.

The WORD Became Flesh

Read Luke 22:14-20. Jesus tells His disciples, "I have earnestly desired to eat this Passover with you before I suffer." Oddly enough, in these words, you can almost hear joy in Jesus' voice. The observance of the last supper is so often done in a solemn, sorrowful tone, but Jesus' words reveal that something much anticipated was happening in the sharing of the last supper.

What do these words reveal to you about how Jesus viewed His earthly role in God's plan for humanity?

_____

_____

_____

The meal was not about eating supper, it was a covenant ceremony. This moment was the beginning of a new relationship and a new identity for the disciples. As He shared the last supper with His disciples, Jesus was giving His disciples the opportunity to fully respond, in a definitive manner, to His earthly, incarnate mission. Passing the cup could be equated to the moment during a wedding ceremony when the minister asks, "Do you take this woman to be your wife?" Drinking from the cup can be equated with, "I do." No wonder there was such great anticipation on His part.

It is also interesting that Jesus instituted the new covenant while celebrating the Passover. The Passover celebration was not only in honor of God delivering the Israelites out of Egypt, but it was done in recognition of the old covenant.

Let's spend some time looking at this "new covenant," and dig deeper into how and why these two words would change everything. The new covenant is first presented in the book of Jeremiah, chapter 31, and its final presentation is in the book of Hebrews, chapters 8–10. Let's look at the first presentation of the new covenant so that we can establish a basic knowledge of God's definition of the new covenant. The restatement of the covenant from Hebrews 8:7-13 will not be written out in this study, but we will refer to the restatement, and it is highly recommended that you read it as well.

Jeremiah 31:27-34

²⁷ *"Behold, days are coming," declares the LORD, "when I will sow the house of Israel and the house of Judah with the seed of man and with the seed of beast. ²⁸ "As I have watched over them to pluck up, to break down, to overthrow, to destroy and to bring disaster, so I will watch over them to build and to plant," declares the LORD. ²⁹ "In those days they will not say again, 'The fathers have eaten sour grapes, And the children's teeth are set on edge.' ³⁰ "But everyone will die for his own iniquity; each man who eats the sour grapes, his teeth will be set on edge. ³¹ Behold, days are coming," declares the LORD, "when I will make a new covenant with the house of Israel and with the house of Judah, ³² not like the covenant which I made with their fathers in the day I took them by the hand to bring them out of the land of Egypt, My covenant which they broke, although I was a husband to them," declares the LORD. ³³ "But this is the covenant which I will make with the house of Israel after those days," declares the LORD, "I will put My law within them and on their heart I will write it; and I will be their God, and they shall be My people. ³⁴ "They will not teach again, each man his neighbor and each man his brother, saying, 'Know the LORD,' for they will all know Me, from the least of them to the greatest of them," declares the LORD, "for I will forgive their iniquity, and their sin I will remember no more."*

As you read verses 27 and 28, it is important to understand that the use of the phrase "seed of man" is <u>not</u> a reference to Jesus. The historical context here is very important. This prophecy was given to Jeremiah while Israel and Judah were being held in Babylonian captivity. The nation and their animals had been depleted. God, through Jeremiah, is telling the nation, that He is going "to build and to plant" them. This is about a literal restoration of the Jews to Jerusalem.

As you continue reading into verses 29 and 30, God, through Jeremiah, is telling His people about how wickedness will be dealt with from that point forward. This is a declaration of the end of multiple generations being cursed for the wickedness of an ancestor. (This doesn't mean that

The Covenant Maker Is a Covenant Keeper

sins aren't taught and passed on from generation to generation, rather, this is about consequences.)

Read Ezekiel 14:12-20. Ezekiel and Jeremiah were contemporaries. What does God reveal through Ezekiel about the righteous? What sort of responsibility is placed on the individual?

_____

_____

_____

Read Luke 17:2; Matthew 18:6; Mark 9:42. While your own righteousness is insufficient for saving your children, what do these verses tell you about leading your children into sin?

_____

_____

_____

Read Hebrews 8:7-8,13. The writer of Hebrews tells us that the old covenant is made obsolete by the new covenant. God tells Jeremiah, ". . . I will make a new covenant with the house of Israel and Judah, not like the covenant I made with their fathers . . ." (Jer. 31:31-32). Why was a new covenant necessary?

_____

_____

_____

Read Acts 10:44-48; Galatians 3:6-9,13-14,16-18,27-29. In verse 31, God, through Jeremiah, states ". . . I will make a new covenant with the house of Israel and with the house of Judah . . ." Are non-Jewish people a part of this covenant? If so, how?

_____

_____

_____

God never intended the covenant with Abraham to be exclusively for the nation of Israel. His initial charge for Abram reveals this, "And in you all the families of the earth will be blessed" (Gen. 12:3).

God used the nation of Israel to reveal who He is and to draw a contrast of what it means to be His versus what it means to be of the world. Throughout the Old Testament history of Israel, the nation managed to exemplify both sides of the contrast. At times, they fell into judgment as a result of rebellion. At other times, they aligned themselves with God and His statutes, and were blessed for it.

Before we move on, let's visit a topic that was mentioned in the Abrahamic covenant. This is not being brought up to stir up controversy, but instead to make a point. In discussion of the Abrahamic covenant, I pointed out how many Arab Muslims trace their lineage through Ishmael or Ham. Furthermore, Jews trace their lineage through Isaac. With a very different understanding of the line through which the Abrahamic covenant was passed down, there has been a long-time struggle over the land that is currently occupied by the Jews, known as Israel or to the Muslims, Palestine (AKA Canaan). Regardless of your view of through whom the covenant was passed down, God's words to Abraham are the same, "all families of the earth will be blessed."

Understanding Inheritance

Non-mathematical people, please forgive me, but a little math must be done here. Israel (Canaan) encompasses approximately 8000 sq. miles, not counting the Gaza strip. When we realize God promised that all families of the earth would be blessed through Abraham, the current struggle for land seems rather futile. There are seven billion people currently residing on earth. If we take seven billion and divide it by eight thousand, we come up with a figure of 875,000 people living in each square mile. That sounds a bit cramped to me.

The understanding of inheritance and blessing should not be about land. The blessing we share in is a divine inheritance. It isn't about material things at all. Instead, it is about being with God. He is the inheritance, His presence. It isn't about how God can bless us with material goods. It is about Him and only Him. God invites us into His presence, not so that He can give us stuff. He invites us into His presence, because we are only complete when we are with Him.

God, through Jeremiah, states, ". . . My covenant which they broke, although I was a husband to them . . ." (Jer. 31:32), but this seemingly stands in contrast to the presentation in Hebrews. In Hebrews, God, through the apostle, states, ". . . For they did not continue in My covenant, and I did not care for them . . ." (Heb. 8:9). It may be tempting to use these words to refute the infallibility of Scripture, but it was more likely an opportunity for God to help us understand the role of Christ with the church.

Read Colossians 1:18. What do these words, which are more complimentary than contrasting, reveal about God's plan for Christ and the church?

_____

_____

_____

The New Covenant

Read Ezekiel 36:27; 1 Corinthians 3:16; 1 Corinthians 6:19. God originally wrote His Law on stone tablets. Here, in verse 33, He promises to write His Law on our hearts. How does God write His law on our hearts?

_____

_____

_____

Read Exodus 40:34. The passage in Jeremiah reveals that the new covenant will be unlike the old covenant. As you reflect on verse 33, what is different about God's dwelling place?

_____

_____

_____

The dwelling place of God shifting from a tabernacle to the individual hearts of humans should not go unnoticed. So often, we are happy to acknowledge the saving power of Jesus Christ, yet we still consider God to be an external being. It is true that God is external, but because He is omnipresent, in the Holy Spirit, He is internalized in the hearts of those who are in Christ. It is in this way that He transforms our lives, as He transforms our hearts.

Consider Moses' words in Exodus, "The glory of the LORD filled the tabernacle" (Ex. 40:34). How is that statement reflected by the indwelling of the Holy Spirit in your heart?

_____

_____

_____

Read Exodus 6:6-7. Although there are some huge differences, as you read Jeremiah 31:33, what will remain unchanged from the old covenant to the new covenant?

_____

_____

_____

Read 1 John 2:27; John 14:26; Luke 12:12, 1 Corinthians 2:13; John 16:13-14. Jeremiah tells us, "They will not teach again . . . for they will all know Me" (Jer. 31:34). While it is still acceptable and highly recommended that we familiarize ourselves with God's written Law, how do we learn the Law in such a way that it is internalized? How will we know that what we are learning is truth?

_____

_____

_____

The Holy Spirit will always glorify Christ Jesus and disclose truth to those who are in Christ. God's Word is truth (John 17:17), and the Holy Spirit will not contradict the Word of God. We know the Holy Spirit will not contradict the Word of God because it was the Holy Spirit that was dwelling in the writers of the Scriptures (1 Pet. 1:10-12). In other words, the Holy Spirit knows the Scriptures fully.

When you are struggling with your understanding of God's Word, spending time in prayer, allowing the Holy Spirit to guide you is always of utmost importance. As you pray, pray expectantly that the Holy Spirit will guide you in your studies of the Word. Remember, just because you think something, doesn't mean it is of the Holy Spirit. The Holy Spirit speaks and reveals truth in God's Word. Like the Word of God, the Holy Spirit is not bound by your opinion. That said, we all enter into Scripture with bias. Submitting your heart to the Word is the first step, allowing the Holy Spirit to reveal His truth and greater depth to you is the second step.

Holy Spirit Discloses Identity

If we take time to consider that the Holy Spirit discloses truth to us, we may wonder how that is manifested in our day-to-day lives. Let's take a moment to apply this to temptation and sin. If you think about temptation and sin, you will see that between the moment of temptation and the actual step into the moment of sin, there is a moment of pause. This is the moment where a decision is made either to step away from temptation or step into sin. This moment of pause is where the Holy Spirit is disclosing truth. What is the responsibility of those who are in Christ when we reach the moment of pause?

_____

It is obvious that we are going to say something like, "step away from temptation" or "don't sin." What may be less obvious is this: we are to respond to the Holy Spirit and follow truth. Temptation is never about the sin, but is instead about your identity. When we choose sin, we are choosing a false and sinful identity. When we choose to step away from temptation and not sin, we are choosing our true identity in Christ.

The New Covenant

Based on Jeremiah 31:34, does social status play a part in whether or not God reveals Himself to a person?

Read Matthew 26:26-28. In Matthew, we see the words, "poured out for many for the forgiveness of sins." (Matt. 26:28) How did Jesus accomplish God's promise from Jeremiah 31:34?

_____

_____

_____

Perhaps the most comforting aspects of the new covenant are the final statements, "for I will forgive their iniquity, and their sins I will remember no more" (Jer. 31:34). Because God's Word is truth, there is great comfort in these words, however, many struggle with one or both statements.

Let's break this down. How do you respond to these two phrases:

"for I will forgive their iniquity"

"their sins I will remember no more"

How often do we accept forgiveness, give the sin over to Jesus on the cross, and then return to the cross to retrieve it and carry that sin around just a little while longer? By remembering our sins and trying to carry them once more, we aren't really accepting forgiveness. We are only accepting the idea of forgiveness. In other words, we accept it intellectually, but emotionally it is still there, and those sins remain a part of our identity. We remain in a state of being defined by our past and enslaved to a sin that we once gave to Christ. This failure to accept forgiveness is essentially a return to the Law. If this state of being was Christ's intention for us, He would have stayed in Heaven.

Ratification   Earlier in this lesson, we read that the new covenant rendered the old covenant obsolete. You may be wondering why the new covenant was necessary, and for that matter, what makes this one binding if the old covenant could be made obsolete? For better understanding, let's look at the explanation the writer of Hebrews offers in the two chapters (chs. 9 and 10) following the presentation of the new covenant.

Hebrews 9:1-5

¹Now even the first covenant had regulations of divine worship and the earthly sanctuary. ²For there was a tabernacle prepared, the outer one, in which were the lampstand and the table and the sacred bread; this is called the holy place. ³Behind the second veil there was a tabernacle which is called the Holy of Holies, ⁴having a golden altar of incense and the ark of the covenant covered on all sides with gold, in which was a golden jar holding the manna, and Aaron's rod which budded, and the tables of the covenant; ⁵and above it were the cherubim of glory overshadowing the mercy seat; but of these things we cannot now speak in detail.

Read Revelation 4:2-9 and 5:8. In Revelation, John enters the presence of Almighty God, sitting on the throne. What similarities do you see between the tabernacle, which held the Ark of the Covenant, and the space John entered (often referred to as the "throne room") to view God upon the throne?

_____

_____

_____

_____

_____

_____

What separated the inner tabernacle (the Holy of Holies) from the outer tabernacle, likewise, what separated the outer tabernacle from the outer world?

As you think about a veil, what words or images come to mind?

_____

_____

Hebrews 9:6-10

⁶Now when these things have been so prepared, the priests are continually entering the outer tabernacle performing the divine worship, ⁷but into the second, only the high priest enters once a year, not without taking blood, which he offers for himself and for the sins of the people committed in ignorance. ⁸The Holy Spirit is signifying this, that the way into the holy place has not yet been disclosed while the outer tabernacle is still standing, [9]which is a symbol for the present time. Accordingly both gifts and sacrifices are offered which cannot make the worshiper perfect in conscience, [10]since they relate only to food and drink and various washings, regulations for the body imposed until a time of reformation.

Hebrews 10:1-4

[1]*For the Law, since it has only a shadow of the good things to come and not the very form of things, can never, by the same sacrifices which they offer continually year by year, make perfect those who draw near. [2]Otherwise, would they not have ceased to be offered, because the worshipers, having once been cleansed, would no longer have had consciousness of sins? [3]But in those sacrifices there is a reminder of sins year by year. [4]For it is impossible for the blood of bulls and goats to take away sins.*

Who was allowed to enter the tabernacle?

The high priest entered the Holy of Holies only one time per year. How often did the priests enter the tabernacle to perform worship and offer sacrifices? What similarity does this hold to the throne room in Revelation 4?

_____

_____

_____

When the high priest offered the annual sacrifice, for which sins was he sacrificing?

_____

_____

_____

There are times when we knowingly sin, but there are also sins we commit without knowledge and premeditated intent. Perhaps these sins are a part of our natural habits and, therefore, they don't really seem unnatural to us. Perhaps they are a part of our cultural norms. Regardless of knowledge and intent, they fall outside the scope of God's will for us.

Were the sacrifices offered by the priests, or the high priest, sufficient to take away sins?

_____

_____

_____

The question then may arise, "What was the point of the sacrifices, and did they have any power at all?" The power of these sacrifices was based in the show of faith in God's Word and the hope of redemption, as God had promised the nation of Israel. The people were in a constant state of having to remember their sins.[8]

The writer of Hebrews states, "The Holy Spirit *is* signifying this, that the way into the holy place has not yet been disclosed while the outer tabernacle is still standing" (Heb. 9:8). Read Matthew 27:50-51. What happened at Christ's death that revealed the way into the holy place?   **Unveiling**

_____

_____

_____

Hebrews 9:11-14

[11]*But when Christ appeared as a high priest of the good things to come, He entered through the greater and more perfect tabernacle, not made with hands, that is to say, not of this creation;* [12]*and not through the blood of goats and calves, but through His own blood, He entered the holy place once for all, having obtained eternal redemption.* [13]*For if the blood of goats and bulls and the ashes of a heifer sprinkling those who have been defiled sanctify for the cleansing of the flesh,* [14]*how much more will the blood of Christ, who through the eternal Spirit offered Himself without blemish to God, cleanse your conscience from dead works to serve the living God?*

After the death of Christ, the way into the holy place was revealed. It was then that, "He entered the holy place once for all, having obtained eternal redemption." It was at this moment that our salvation was secured as He entered "through His own blood" to "cleanse your conscience from dead works to serve the living God" (Heb. 9:12,14). In other words, Jesus entered the holy place to set you free from your sins so that He, **and you**, would remember them no more and sacrificing animals and burnt offerings could be a thing of the past.

The New Covenant

Hebrews 10:5-9

[5]*Therefore, when He comes into the world, He says, "SACRIFICE AND OFFERING YOU HAVE NOT DESIRED, BUT A BODY YOU HAVE PREPARED FOR ME;* [6]*IN WHOLE BURNT OFFERINGS AND sacrifices FOR SIN YOU HAVE TAKEN NO PLEASURE.* [7]*"THEN I SAID, 'BEHOLD, I HAVE COME (IN THE SCROLL OF THE BOOK IT IS WRITTEN OF ME) TO DO YOUR WILL, O GOD.'"* [8]*After saying above, "SACRIFICES AND OFFERINGS AND WHOLE BURNT OFFERINGS AND sacrifices FOR SIN YOU HAVE NOT DESIRED, NOR HAVE YOU TAKEN PLEASURE in them" (which are offered according to the Law),* [9]*then He said, "BEHOLD, I HAVE COME TO DO YOUR WILL." He takes away the first in order to establish the second.*

For You   Read Genesis 3:21 and Jeremiah 7:21-23. Because of the sin of Adam and Eve in the garden, God sacrificed the first animal in history in order to make clothes, as Adam and Eve were ashamed after sinning. Instead of sacrificing animals, what was God's intention, from the beginning, for mankind?

_____

_____

_____

At no time did God ever desire our sacrifices. It needs to be understood that sacrifices were never for God, they were, instead, for us. He didn't need them. Because of sin, we needed them, and so, He sacrificed for us. Instead of sacrifices, God desired our obedience, not out of subjugation, but out of faithfulness and loyalty to a loving Creator.

Not only did Christ bring an end to sacrificing animals and burnt offerings, He secured our forgiveness and our inheritance. We read earlier in the lesson about the inheritance for the descendants of Abraham and read that we have a spirit of adoption and a claim to that inheritance through Christ Jesus. The writer of Hebrews explains how this inheritance was legally secured to be passed on to us through Christ.

Hebrews 9:15-22

[15]*For this reason He is the mediator of a new covenant, so that, since a death has taken place for the redemption of the transgressions that were committed under the first covenant, those who have been called may receive the promise of the eternal inheritance.* [16]*For where a covenant is, there must of necessity be the death of the one who made it.* [17]*For a covenant is valid only when men are dead, for it is never in force while the one who made it lives.* [18]*Therefore even the first covenant was not inaugurated*

without blood. ¹⁹For when every commandment had been spoken by Moses to all the people according to the Law, he took the blood of the calves and the goats, with water and scarlet wool and hyssop, and sprinkled both the book itself and all the people, ²⁰saying, "THIS IS THE BLOOD OF THE COVENANT WHICH GOD COMMANDED YOU." ²¹And in the same way he sprinkled both the tabernacle and all the vessels of the ministry with the blood. ²²And according to the Law, one may almost say, all things are cleansed with blood, and without shedding of blood there is no forgiveness.

To better understand this, it is helpful to know that the Greek word for covenant, used in verses 16 and 17, can also be translated "testament" or "will" (as in, last will and testament). Try reading verses 16 and 17 again with the words, "will and testament" in place of the word covenant.

Once you read it with the replacement words, "will and testament," this becomes fairly self-explanatory. As explained earlier in the lesson, covenants establish relationship and relationships require responsibility. In covenant, God assumed the responsibility of caring for His people. Because of sin and disobedience to His Law, we made it so He "did not care for us" (Heb. 8:9). It was then that it became His responsibility to not only sacrifice for us, but to become the sacrifice for us and enter the holy place through His blood. Believing this and knowing this, our response to God's kingdom responsibility is obedience, springing forth from faithfulness and love. To understand this better, let's read what the writer of Hebrews had to say about Christ entering the holy place.

Hebrews 9:23-28

²³Therefore it was necessary for the copies of the things in the heavens to be cleansed with these, but the heavenly things themselves with better sacrifices than these. ²⁴For Christ did not enter a holy place made with hands, a mere copy of the true one, but into heaven itself, now to appear in the presence of God for us; ²⁵nor was it that He would offer Himself often, as the high priest enters the holy place year by year with blood that is not his own. ²⁶Otherwise, He would have needed to suffer often since the foundation of the world; but now once at the consummation of the ages He has been manifested to put away sin by the sacrifice of Himself. ²⁷And inasmuch as it is appointed for men to die once and after this comes judgment, ²⁸so Christ also, having been offered once to bear the sins of many, will appear a second time for salvation without reference to sin, to those who eagerly await Him.

"For Christ did not enter a holy place made with hands . . ." The writer of Hebrews is referring to the earthly tabernacle, and goes on to refer to it as, "a mere copy of the true one." The writer then tells us that the true tabernacle is "heaven itself" and that Jesus appeared "in the presence of God for us" (Heb. 9:24).

**Everything
I AM,
Is Yours**

God was in the Holy of Holies when the high priest would enter. Therefore, the high priest was in the presence of God. However, it may be helpful to read Exodus 33:19-23 for a clearer understanding of His presence in the Holy of Holies. Read Exodus 33:19-23. Was the high priest in the full presence of God's glory?

_____

_____

_____

In Hebrews, the writer tells us Jesus appeared "in the presence of God for us" and that He did so in "heaven itself." Earlier in the lesson, we looked at the similarities of the tabernacle and the place in heaven where John saw the throne of God. Let's return one more time to Revelation, where the veil has been removed and John bears witness to Jesus Christ appearing before the throne of Almighty God for us.

✢ Read Revelation 5 ✢

Jesus, the "Lion from the tribe of Judah," (Rev. 5:5) walked this earth without blemish. Yet, He offered Himself as a sacrifice and returned to heaven. Having done so, His first appearance before His Almighty Father, who sat upon His throne in His full and radiant glory, was as that of a Lamb who was slain. A more humble picture I cannot imagine. In His humility, He was deemed "Worthy . . . to receive power and riches and wisdom and might and honor and glory and blessing" (Rev. 5:12). It was in this power that He calls us into new life, and into a new identity.

Hebrews 10:19-25

[19] *Therefore, brethren, since we have confidence to enter the holy place by the blood of Jesus, [20] by a new and living way which He inaugurated for us through the veil, that is, His flesh, [21] and since we have a great priest over the house of God, [22] let us draw near with a sincere heart in full assurance of faith, having our hearts sprinkled clean from an evil conscience and our bodies washed with pure water. [23] Let us hold fast the confession of our hope without wavering, for He who promised is faithful; [24] and let us consider how to stimulate one another to love and good deeds, [25] not forsaking our own assembling together, as is the habit of some, but encouraging one another; and all the more as you see the day drawing near.*

What can we now do with confidence?

_____

What has His blood done to our hearts?

_____

What are we to do with one another?

_____

The holy place is a place reserved for priests. Read Revelation 5:10 and 1 Peter 2:9. What is your new identity in Christ?

_____

_____

The apostle Paul has some words for Titus, the church at Galatia, and us, regarding the results brought forth by Christ's actions. Read Titus 2:11-13 and Galatians 5:1. Answer the following questions:

What has appeared or been revealed?

_____

What has it brought along or carried with it?

_____

What does it instruct or teach us to do?

_____

For what does it instruct us to look or wait?

_____

For what purpose does grace and freedom exist?

_____

_____

What effect does grace have in your life and how you live?

_____

_____

_____

While this study is long enough without the following information, it would be a great disservice to fail to mention that there are consequences for failure to accept the blood of Jesus and receive forgiveness. Hebrews 10:26-31 paints an unpleasant picture for those who fall back into judgment.

Into All the Nations . . . You. Go.

Read Matthew 28:19-20. At the beginning of this chapter, it was stated that the disciples "knew they were entering into a new type of relationship with God as they drank from the cup. They also knew that doing so would bring on new responsibilities." They knew it. Do you?

Closing Reflections

Read Hebrews 11:1-2; Genesis 15:6; Romans 10:8-10; Galatians 3:6-9. Although salvation is open to everyone, not everyone is saved. There is one element that is essential to salvation. What do these verses reveal about righteousness and salvation?

Read Philippians 2:1-11. In verse 5, Paul states, "Have this attitude in yourselves which was also in Christ Jesus." According to verses 1-4 and verses 6-8, how is this attitude exemplified?

As you read verses 9-11 in Philippians 2, what purpose do you see being accomplished? What do you see as your kingdom responsibility?

Join the Conversation on:

Facebook: facebook.com/Thecovenantschristandyou Like and Post your thoughts on The New Covenant to which Christ calls you.

or

Twitter: @CovChristU Tweet your thoughts on The New Covenant to which Christ calls you.

Engaging Others:

Tweet it, Post it, Pin it, or Instagram a picture of an empty chair, perhaps at a table. Invite others by saying, "There's a place for you…" or "There's an empty seat at the table for you…" Tweet it to @CovChristU or Tag the Facebook page.

Suggested Hashtags
#Discipleship #ChristFollower #BibleStudy #SmallGroup #Evangelism #Relevant #Jesus

If you haven't done so, it is time to invite. By now, I hope you understand that *The Covenants, Christ, and You* is not about my opinions and observations. It isn't a book asking you to simply ponder Scripture without clear direction, but is instead a book that uses Scripture to examine Scripture. *The Covenants, Christ, and You* is a resource for discipling others and directing them to greater truths in God's Holy Word. I do hope this book has blessed you as much as it blessed me in the writing, study, and prayer. I cannot reach everyone in the world, and neither can you, but you and I can both reach a few, and if they reach a few, and if they reach a few, and if they reach a few…. It's how 12 became 2.1 billion.

Now that you have completed your study, please return to the Preface at the beginning of the book and read the Personal Bible Study, Transformation Group and Discipleship Training, and Final Thoughts sections. Make sure you complete the challenge I presented in the Final Thoughts section.

Notes

[1] Thanks to Adam Scutti, who wanted no recognition for this illustration.

[2] Thanks to James Sharp for getting me on the suzerain-vassal train.

[3] Definition retrieved from http://www.cognitiveatlas.org/concept/deception.

[4] Thanks to Andrew Kirschner for this explanation.

[5] Israelites were known as Hebrews.

[6] Levites were the descendants of Jacob's son Levi.

[7] Boa, Kenneth D et al. New *American Standard Bible.* (La Habra, Calif.: The Lockman Foundation, 1977) *The New Open Bible Study Edition.* (Nashville: Thomas Nelson Publishers, 1990) *87-88.*

[8] Jamieson, Robert et al. *A Commentary, Critical, Practical, and Explanatory on the Old and New Testaments* at http://biblehub.com/commentaries/jfb/genesis/1.htm, February 27, 2015.

References

Boa, Kenneth D.; Broomall, Wick; Criswell, W.A.; Farstad, Arthur, L.; Fink, Paul R.; Hoke, Donald E.; Knight, George; Lee, R. G.; Lorenzen, Myles; McInteer, Jim Bill; Unger, Merrill F.; Ward, C. M.; White, William; Wilkinson, Bruce H.; Williams, Neal D.; Willmington, Harold L. *New American Standard Bible.* La Habra, Calif.: The Lockman Foundation, 1977. *The New Open Bible Study Edition.* Nashville: Thomas Nelson Publishers, 1990.

Clark, Adam. *Commentary on the Bible.* http://biblehub.com/commentaries/clarke/genesis/1.htm, February 27, 2015.

Gill, John. *Exposition of the Entire Bible.* http://biblehub.com/commentaries/gill/genesis/1.htm, February 27, 2015.

Henry, Matthew. *Concise Commentary on the Whole Bible.* http://biblehub.com/commentaries/mhc/genesis/1.htm, February 27, 2015.

Jamieson, Robert; Fausset, A.R.; Brown, David. *A Commentary, Critical, Practical, and Explanatory on the Old and New Testaments.* http://biblehub.com/commentaries/jfb/genesis/1.htm, February 27, 2015.

Nisbet, James (compiled and edited by). *The Pulpit Commentary, Electronic Database.* http://biblehub.com/commentaries/pulpit/genesis/1.htm, February 27, 2015.

Spader, Dann. *Walking as Jesus Walked: Making Disciples the Way Jesus Did.* Chicago: Moody Publisher, 2011.

http://biblehub.com, February 27, 2015.

http://www.cognitiveatlas.org/concept/deception, February 27, 2015

Acknowledgements

First and foremost, thank You, Father God, for meeting me at my computer each day of this process. Thank You for Your enduring patience with, and abundant grace for, a man who just doesn't get it all the time. I'm so thankful for the ways You have revealed Yourself to me. May this book honor You and may You be glorified wherever it may be.

To Keri Jane, the most amazing woman in my life, thank you for your enduring patience with, and abundant grace for, a man who just doesn't get it all the time. You have been the deliverer and picture of God's love in my life for many years now.

Thanks to Boyce Mouton for your encouragement and time with this manuscript throughout the process.

Thanks to Adam Scutti. Dude! Thanks for your input, support, encouragement, and friendship.

Thanks to Andrew Kirschner. You were the right man for the job and I so very much appreciate your contribution to this book. Thanks for challenging me during content editing.

Thanks to Shy Rees. Your thoughtful and meticulous editing saved me so much time.

Special thanks to Dan Rees for capturing and creatively expanding the vision of the books layout during typesetting. Your attention to detail and thoughtfulness took things to a new level.

Special thanks to Naomi Miller for stepping up with some fantastic art work for each chapter."

Thanks to my parents, Kay Churchill, Steve and Roxanne Churchill, who have supported me in my decision to pursue a career change. I know you're praying for me and my family.

Thanks to Denise Cochran (Aunt Denny) for going through this study in its roughest phase. Much has changed because of your input.

Thanks to Jason Ansley, Jeff Goldammer, Darren Dishman, Justin Avery, and James and April Billings for engaging with me and asking how things are going, never shying away from the elephant in the room. Jeff, I'm sorry, but I never got Big Earl to review the book.

Thanks to James Sharp and Eric Rath for the encouraging words.

Thanks to Jim Shelburne, your leadership during my time in Amarillo set me on the path to keep pursuing God regardless of my circumstance. Your writing has inspired me for years.

To my daughters, Lydia and Julia. Thanks for all the hugs and snuggles, smiles and laughter. I'm so thankful for every moment with you, little ones. May the Word of God bless you, strengthen you, uplift you, inspire you, and always be at the center of your lives.

To my in-laws, Bob and Joan McCasland, and all of KJ's sisters, thanks for praying for us, and for your support. Bob, you probably don't know this, but I have learned more about prayer from you then you can ever imagine. Thanks!

About the Author

Ryan Churchill is new to publishing, but not writing, lesson planning or teaching. He recently resigned from the professional teaching field to pursue writing. While working on his master's degree, he was a co-leader of a small group Bible study, where he often found himself tweaking studies with knowledge-building questions to fill in the gaps. The opportunity to lead Bible studies gave Ryan a deeper and deeper desire to know more about the Bible. After completing his master's degree, Ryan found himself in a very time-consuming career, and instead of learning more about the Bible, he moved further and further away from God's Word.

God kept calling, and one of the tools he used was a book about a man who fell in love with God. After reading *Blue Like Jazz*, by Donald Miller, Ryan realized that knowing about the Bible wasn't as important as knowing God. Furthermore, the Bible (God's Word) is the way to get on the path to knowing Him.

In addition to research skills he learned in graduate school, Ryan brings his understanding of sequential learning and Socratic methodology to this wonderful study of the Biblical covenants. With sixteen years of teaching, Ryan honed his skills in using questions to establish and expand knowledge and deepen understanding.

In writing each chapter of this book, Ryan entered the topics with a fully open mind and open heart. Understanding that bias is a natural effect of prior knowledge, he wrestled with ideas, striving to take nothing for granted. Ryan's pathway to worship is God's Word. The last several months of developing *The Covenants, Christ, and You* were filled with moments of incredible worship as God revealed Himself, His Word, and His Truth to a guy sitting at his computer (and iPad), studying and praying over Scripture, and staring at a word processing program. To God alone . . . Glory.

Recommended Reading List

The following books have inspired me and challenged my walk in the past year. Not only did Dann Spader's book inspire and challenge me, it was paradigm shifting.

Walking as Jesus Walked: Making Disciples the Way Jesus Did by Dann Spader

The Master Plan of Evangelism by Robert E. Coleman

Fresh Wind, Fresh Fire by Jim Cymbala

62532449R00067

Made in the USA
Lexington, KY
10 April 2017